Opera Biographies

This is a volume in the
Arno Press collection

Opera Biographies

Advisory Editor
ANDREW FARKAS

Associate Editor
W.R. MORAN

See last pages of this volume
for complete list of titles

THE LIFE OF JENNY LIND

[Jenny Maria Catherine Goldschmidt] Maude

ARNO PRESS
A New York Times Company
New York / 1977

Editorial Supervision: ANDREA HICKS

Reprint Edition 1977 by Arno Press Inc.

Reprinted from a copy in
The Princeton University Library

OPERA BIOGRAPHIES
ISBN for complete set: 0-405-09666-6
See last pages of this volume for titles.

Manufactured in the United States of America

Publisher's Note: The frontispiece has been reproduced in black and white in this edition.

Library of Congress Cataloging in Publication Data

Maude, Jenny Maria Catherine Goldschmidt.
The life of Jenny Lind.

(Opera biographies)
Reprint of the 1926 ed. published by Cassell, London.
1. Lind-Goldschmidt, Jenny Maria, 1820-1887.
2. Singers--Sweden--Biography. I. Title.
ML420.L7M2 1977 782.1'092'4 [B] 76-29953
ISBN 0-405-09694-1

THE LIFE OF JENNY LIND

JENNY LIND IN "LA FIGLIA DEL REGGIMENTO."

From a Baxter Print.

THE LIFE
OF JENNY LIND

BRIEFLY TOLD BY HER DAUGHTER
MRS RAYMOND MAUDE, O.B.E.

WITH A COLOUR FRONTISPIECE
AND 16 PLATES

CASSELL AND COMPANY, LTD
London, Toronto, Melbourne and Sydney

First Published 1926

Printed in Great Britain

PREFACE

MY mother died in 1887, and for three years after her death my father, Otto Goldschmidt, made many journeys, and took immense pains to collect documents and material for the Memoir, the writing of which he confided to Canon Scott Holland on the social, and to Mr. Rockstro on the musical and technical side. The Memoir was published by Mr. Murray, originally in two volumes, and later condensed into one volume. Both editions are now out of print, and there is no life of my mother available, except in musical dictionaries or encyclopædias. My father, who survived my mother for twenty years, during that time was able to answer any inquiries but did not desire to continue his wife's Life after the date of her marriage, as he would have figured in it himself very largely.

In view of the still constant reference to, and use of her name, I have compiled this little book, in a lighter vein than the old Memoir, from many documents in my possession, aided by my own recollections.

JENNY M. C. MAUDE.

CONTENTS

LIST OF PLATES

THE LIFE OF JENNY LIND

CHAPTER I

1820–1840

THE name of Jenny Lind was a household word in the days of Queen Victoria; she came to power at much the same age, and about the same date as the Queen, not by right of birth, but by right of genius and hard work.

At the present day we are constantly finding mention of her friendships, and doings, in the records of social life in the last century, as well as references to her Art by musical writers. There is, however, no consecutive and authoritative story of her life since the Memoir published soon after her death in 1887, went out of print.

Jenny Lind was born on October 6, 1820, in Stockholm, of middle-class parents, her mother being a well-educated woman a good deal older than her father. He was Nicholas Jonas Lind, only twenty-two years old, and seems to have been a rather irresponsible young man, the possessor of a good voice, but little else. The cares of the household therefore fell on Mme. Lind, who turned her good education to account by opening a day-school for girls. She had been married before, but divorced her husband, retaining the custody of a daughter, nine years old at the time of Jenny's birth. One can understand that a baby was not a convenient addition to a busy household, and shortly after her birth Jenny was put out to nurse with a Mme. Ferndal, who was the wife of the organist and parish clerk in the village of Ed-Sollentuna, about fifteen miles from Stockholm. In those days that distance represented the depth of the country, and it is probable that the intense love Jenny Lind ever retained for country sights, sounds, and the smell of trees dates from her earliest consciousness and it may be also that she imbibed music from the sound of the organ at the same time.

At the age of four the child came home to her family, of whom her maternal grandmother, Fru Tengmark, was an important member, and she all along gave the child the love and encouragement of which the mother's less genial nature seemed incapable. Fru Tengmark was a very religious woman, and early imbued her little granddaughter with her own beliefs. It was she who made the astonishing discovery of the tiny child picking out, on the old spinet in the attic, a tune which passing soldiers played, and then hiding under the piano in fear of reproof.

With the discovery and encouragement of her gifts, Jenny began to sing everything she heard, and sing with every step she took, and happily these steps led her to the notice of someone who could help her, a Mlle. Lundberg. She was a dancer at the Royal Opera, and she induced Count Puke, the director, and Croelius, the chief singing master, to hear the child sing. These gentlemen were so struck with her voice and intelligence that they overlooked her shy and plain exterior, as well as the fact that she was only nine years old, and consented to admit her as a pupil of the Royal Theatre School.

At first it looked as if the child's family would not overcome their religious objections to a stage career, but eventually they saw the great advantage of the fine education she would receive, and they consented.

At the age of nine years, therefore, under very strict conditions, Jenny Lind became the pupil of the Royal Theatre School and it became the scene and centre of her life.

There she found a nursery for her talents, a school for learning and discipline, where she was watched over with interest and authority. The theatre was subsidized by the Court Civil List and was directed and controlled by the Court Chamberlain. It stood in the heart of Stockholm, close to the North Bridge, and overlooked the wide basin of the North Stream. It was a fine building, and had good airy rooms for the girls, of whom Jenny Lind was the youngest. These girls did not live at the school but were boarded out, in carefully chosen homes, and so it came about that Jenny was boarded out with her own mother under a contract which the directors drew up. This constituted Jenny an actress-pupil of the Royal Theatre, and could only be rescinded by the directors when, through her after-efforts, she should have made restitution for the care and expense bestowed on her education. Very precise details as to her teaching, and the payments for her board and pocket money, were gone into, and the contract is impressive as requiring the "full teaching for an educated woman." There is in that phrase a distinct ideal. Elocution, dancing and deportment, the piano and singing, as well as languages and the usual school subjects, are included in the curriculum, the memory of which was re-echoed fifty years later in Mme. Goldschmidt's proposals for her pupils at the Royal College of Music in London.

She herself learnt to move, walk, and hold herself with perfect poise and dignity, and no one can fail to remember the records of how she stood on the concert platform when she sang. There was a certain amount of conversational French in use in Stockholm at that time owing to the Royal Family's French descent ; still she thought it necessary to take special lessons before going to Paris in 1841, and during her enforced rest there she studied Italian and improved her German. English she only learnt during her first stay in England.

As a child Jenny scarred the inside of her left hand while striking fire with a flint, but that did not prevent her from playing the piano with ease, if not with the mastery of a skilled pianist. She improvised well, and part of the charm of her singing of Swedish songs came from the delicious way in which she played the accompaniments. All these adjuncts to her vocal achievements are as attributable to her early, steady schooling, as to her natural gifts.

So Jenny had settled down with what seemed good hopes of happiness, and a career had taken definite shape. The only cloud was the contrast between the interest and cheerfulness of her days at school, and the friction at home, where the narrowness and austerity of outlook affected her nature, and induced a seriousness which she never lost.

The first time her name ever appeared on a playbill was on November 29, 1830, when she was ten years old, in a play called *The Polish Mine.* She took the part of Angela, who had to dance, not sing (!), and she figured as "Élève Jenny Lind."

Croelius, her first singing-master, had been succeeded by Berg, and there is a remarkable account given by the newspaper *Heimdal* of Jenny's progress at the age of twelve. It says, under date April 24, 1832: "Jenny's remarkable musical gift and its precocious development, have made quite a sensation in the circle in which she has appeared, guided by her master, Herr Berg. Her memory is as perfect as it is sure; her receptive powers as quick as they are profound. Everyone is thus both astonished and moved by her singing. She can stand a trial of the most difficult solfeggi, and intricate phrases, without being bewildered, and, whatever turns the improvisations of her master take, she follows, as if they were her own. If this young genius does not ripen too prematurely, there is every reason for expecting to find in her eventually an operatic artist of high rank." This is a fascinating picture of the child of twelve

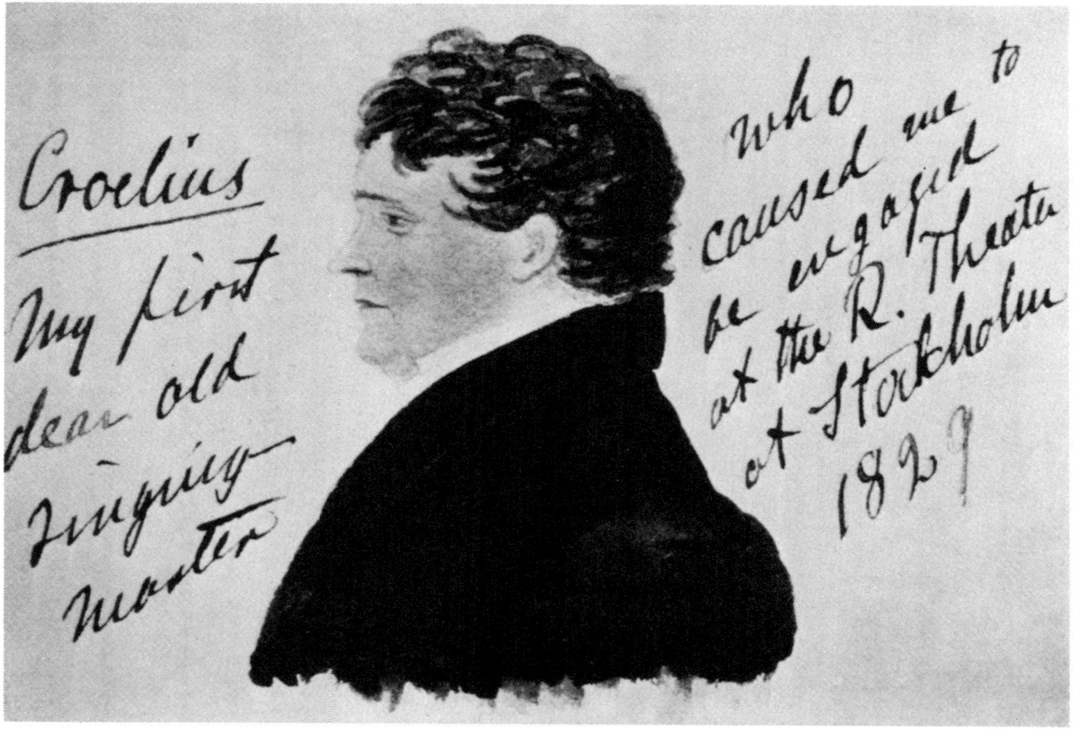

SILHOUETTE PORTRAIT OF CROELIUS.
Inscribed by Jenny Lind.

miraculously following and interpreting her teacher's mind.

To Croelius belongs the merit of first believing in her, but it was Berg who gave her her entire stage training, and he remained her staunch friend to the end of his days. He was also the composer of the song *Fjeran i skug* which Mlle. Lind sang so frequently, and into which she introduced the long-sustained notes for which she was famous.

The newspaper, *Allahanda*, was also taking an interest in this remarkable child, and on one occasion it took the directors to task for allowing one so young to take part in a play of a doubtful kind.

On January 1, 1837, the directors were to decide as to giving Jenny a fixed salary as an actress, and they fixed it at 700 Rix Daler (about £60) a year, and a bonus for each performance. For this she certainly did plenty of work, for she appeared ninety-two times in drama, in twelve new parts, thus amassing much dramatic experience at an early age. By the time she was seventeen she had appeared a hundred and eleven times, in fifteen different plays, as well as her first attempt in the only opera written by Lindblad, which had little success. There is no doubt that during her sixteenth and seventeenth years her singing was intentionally restricted, but it is not true that she lost her voice, or how could she have sung in opera in 1838 and the following years, or given so many concerts to collect funds to go to Paris?

We now come to the year 1838, which was to be the turning-point of Mlle. Lind's life, for on March 7 she made her first serious debut, playing Agathe in Weber's opera *Der Freischütz*. She often said: "I got up that morning one creature, and I went to bed another, for I had found my vocation." All through life Jenny Lind observed that date with a religious solemnity, and would ask others to remember her in their prayers on the day. It was her birthday as an artist. She used to tell how, in studying the part of Agathe with Mme. Erichsen, one of her teachers of whom she was very fond, she one day put forth all her powers with the desire to satisfy her teacher, only to be met with a dead silence. "Am I then so stupid and incapable," she thought, till she saw the tears trickling down Mme. Erichsen's cheeks, and was told, "My child, I have no more to teach you. Do as Nature tells you."

During that year, the *Freischütz* was given nine times, and in between, Jenny played much in drama, appearing altogether seventy-three times for her £60, but in the following year her success bore fruit in an increase of salary to £90, and her operatic parts grew in importance. She appeared as Julia in Spontini's *Vestale*, a part which she greatly enjoyed playing.

But the event of that year (1839) was her first appearance as Alice in *Roberto il Diavolo*, in which part she was destined to win her greatest successes. During the whole of her short operatic career Mlle. Lind sang Alice seventy-three times, of which sixty performances were at Stockholm. Bournonville, a distinguished composer of ballets, in Copenhagen wrote in his "Theatrical Life" of her performance: "She was only eighteen when I first heard her, but had so eminent a talent, that her performance of Alice could be compared to the best I had seen and heard in Paris. Although her voice had not yet reached the high development it afterwards attained, it already possessed the same sympathetic and electrical power which now makes it so irresistible."

During the following three years Jenny Lind upheld the fortune of her theatre, but with growing doubts as to the welfare of her voice, upon which hard work was telling. She felt she needed fresh advice, not only as to her singing but as to her progress in her Art.

In May, 1839, we find Mlle. Lind giving her first concert, on her own behalf, at the Royal Theatre;

she sang a recitative and air from *Anna Bolena* and took part in a duet by Mercadente. In June she was giving a concert in her own name at Upsala, and it was her first, fascinating experience of being escorted home by the students, singing College songs. It was on this occasion that she first met the historian, Geijer, who became a sympathetic friend and admirer. He, as well as other friends, warned her of the danger she was running of overstraining both her vocal and physical powers. She therefore went to Gothenberg, where she rested for the summer, singing now and again but without serious work. Her mother was with her, and in a letter to Mr. Lind she tells him of the interest everywhere shown in their daughter, who received visits from many eminent people and lovers of music. About July 20 there was to be a concert, and the mother laments that the price of the tickets is not to be raised ; a typical instance of the divergence of mind between mother and daughter.

This divergence was becoming more and more marked and serves to explain the approaching decision that Mlle. Lind made, to bring to an end the uncomfortable life in her parents' home. Louise Johannsen had from her early days been a boarder in the Linds' house, and she and Jenny decided to transfer themselves to the house of a well-to-do relative of the Linds, a Fröken Appolonia Lindskog, commonly called "Tante Lona." Her parents could not claim a girl of nineteen from the house of a relative, and later on they consented to allow Jenny and her maid Annette to stay at the Bonde Palace, where the Lindblads had a flat.

Adolf Lindblad was the chief Swedish song-writer of the day; he was a warm friend and admirer of Mlle. Lind and had considerable influence in her artistic and intellectual development; in Mme. Lindblad Jenny found a second mother, much more in sympathy with her character and lofty aims than was her own mother. Though endowed with considerable stubbornness, Jenny Lind was at this period singularly uncertain of herself, and easily unnerved; she needed an atmosphere of affection to give her confidence and save her from the miseries of suspicion and distrust into which she was apt to lapse.

This affection and comfort she found with the Lindblads, and she remained with them until she went to Paris.

The year 1840 must have therefore been a much happier one. Mlle. Lind only appeared in opera, never in drama, and she added the two important rôles of Donna Anna in *Don Giovanni* and Lucia in *Lucia di Lammermoor* to her repertoire. In Lucia she created a furore, and sang it twenty-eight times in the year.

At Whitsuntide, Mlle. Lind again visited Upsala, and Geijer again showed the interest in her which he shared with Lindblad. The newspaper *Correspondenten* was writing graceful criticisms of her doings, and for the first time referred to her as "the Nightingale," a name which was destined to cling to her.

In that year, too, Mlle. Lind was made a member of the Swedish Academy of Music and received the compliment of being appointed Court Singer to King Carl Johann. She was received by the whole social world, and enjoyed the society of the most cultivated men and women in Sweden. Her popularity was at its height. The musical authorities of Stockholm had no more to teach her, and the directors of the Royal Theatre were proposing fresh and advanced terms of engagement. But her mind was at work, appraising her success as unwarranted, since she knew she had more to learn, and a higher standard to attain. Geijer's advice had sunk in deep, and she desired to follow it. The celebrated baritone, Belletti, was singing with her at the Opera, and showing her what singing in the Italian style meant, and when consulted as to where such style was to be learnt, he said : " In Paris under Manuel Garcia, the brother of Malibran."

But she had not the means to make the journey to Paris, and resolved to make a tour in Sweden, though it meant still further taxing her voice, between two heavy opera seasons.

In a letter to Louise Johannsen from Malmö she records that the tour was going well, but the travelling was difficult as the roads were bad ; " the wheels often sink a foot in the mud and it is horrid travelling in such atrocious weather." But as soon as she arrived in a town, she was so kindly treated that she felt it wicked to grumble. She closed her letter with a commission which shows how early in life her charities had begun. She had forgotten, before leaving Stockholm, to take a poor sick man his monthly allowance, and asks Louise to take it to him.

Returned to Stockholm, on August 19 Mlle. Lind was singing in *Lucia*, and, in fulfilment of her contract, she sang during the whole of that winter, and the spring of 1841. Her first appearances as Norma were in May of that year, and, in the same part, on June 19, she appeared for the 447th time on the boards of the Royal Theatre since the day when, as a child, she had played Angela, in the drama *The Polish Mine*. The directors had indeed been justified in the venture they had made with the little creature, and she had repaid them well for their confidence.

But now her voice was worn and fatigued; she had done too much. She therefore wrote a notable document to the directors, asking them to defer their offer of a re-engagement for a year, and they agreed to do so.

On June 21, 1841, she gave a Benefit Concert, singing airs from *Norma* and *Anna Bolena*, and ending with a "Farewell," written for the occasion by Lindblad.

Her friends M. and Mme. von Koch arranged for her journey to Paris and lent her a maid.

CHAPTER II

1841–1842

ON July 1, 1841, Mlle. Lind embarked for Lübeck, and continued overland to Hamburg, where she took the boat again to Havre; thence she travelled by diligence to Paris, where she found a comfortable boarding-house kept by a Mme. de Ruffiaque in a street near the Rue neuve des Augustins. She was sure of one friend in Paris, as the wife of her old master, Mme. Berg, was staying there with her little invalid son, Albert. The Chancellor of the Swedish Legation, Herr Blumm, also welcomed her, and showed her much kindness during her stay in the French capital, a practical form being his frequent loan of his manservant as an escort.

Queen Desideria of Sweden had given Mlle. Lind an introduction to her relative, Mme. la Maréchale de Soult, and it was understood that Signor Garcia should be asked to come and hear her sing at the Maréchale's house. She sang some Swedish songs to her own accompaniment, but either from fatigue, or nervousness, or both, she did herself no justice, and made little impression on the assembled guests.

Soon afterwards, Mlle. Lind called on Signor Garcia, by appointment, and requested him to receive her as a pupil. The Maestro put her through the usual tests, and asked her to sing the well-known air from *Lucia.* In this, though she knew every note, she utterly broke down, and needed all her courage to bear his verdict on her tired voice. "Mon enfant vous n'avez plus de voix" (not, as has been so often quoted, "vous n'avez pas de voix"), for he recognized that she had overworked it. He condemned her to absolute abstention from singing, or even from much speaking, for three months.

She was determined not to waste her time, and set about learning Italian, and better French, as well as musical theory and the study of music generally. But it was a time of great misery and home-sickness, as her serious northern nature found little that attracted her in the French capital.

After the first few weeks at Mme. Ruffiaque's, Mlle. Lind moved to cheaper quarters in the house of Mlle. de Puget, a lady who had been educated in Sweden, and so thoroughly understood Swedish mentality that Jenny felt more at home there, and wrote happier letters home to Mme. Lindblad and others. Mlle. Henriette Nissen was another pupil of Garcia's, and when on Mlle. Lind's next visit he found her voice so far restored as to allow study, the two ladies became great friends, and a friendly rivalry sprang up between them. During September Mlle. Lind was having two lessons a week, working again from the beginning, singing scales up and down, slowly, and with great care, practising the shake, and gradually losing her hoarseness. In one of her letters home she wrote that she was feeling very happy in the choice of her new master, that her voice was becoming clear and sonorous, and acquiring more firmness and greater agility. The worst was over, and Garcia was satisfied with her.

Evidently the tuition Mlle. Lind was now receiving was exactly what she needed. Signor Garcia was of infinite use to her in teaching her the management of her breath, the production of her voice, and the blending of her registers, but in that which concerned the higher life of her art she needed no teaching; the knowledge was hers by instinct and inspiration.

During her stay in Paris Mlle. Lind constantly visited the Opera and recorded her impressions in letters home, with frankness and judgment. She wrote of Mme. Persiani with admiration and delight, and followed her performances with great interest. It is evident that, besides striving with all her might to remedy her defects, and master the technical difficulties of singing, under Garcia's guidance, she never forgot for a moment the importance of the dramatic side of her art.

Mlle. Lind's course of study with Garcia lasted ten months, by which time she had learnt all that any master could teach her; and now arose the crucial question—should the finished artist make her debut in Paris, or should she return to Sweden and reappear there in all the glory of her newly acquired powers? She was tortured by indecision, and, in a letter to Mme. Lindblad of April, 1842, she wrote:

I dare not tell you how I long for home; I dare not tell you how far from happy I feel here, but there is one thing in your letter which frightens me. You say that if I come back without having appeared here in public, they will say that I was not fit for Paris, however well I sing. Ho, ho! what will happen then? It might perhaps be better to engage myself as a nursemaid, for it is a very difficult thing to appear here in public. On the stage it would be out of the question; and in the concert room I am at my weakest point. What is wanted here is—admirers. Were I inclined to receive them, all would be smooth sailing. But, there I say—"Stop!"

And to her father she wrote, humorously: "Fancy if I get no engagements! Perhaps I may have to sit on the Djurgård's Common with a little money-box in front of me gathering contributions while I sing. But perhaps they have not quite forgotten me, after all."

This last surmise proved quite correct, as the Stockholm directors wrote and offered her a re-engagement for one or two years at a salary of about £150 in English money per annum, with a bonus for each performance, and costumes provided. This offer Mlle. Lind accepted, for though she knew by this time her greater value, she desired to show her gratitude to her Alma Mater and return to her beloved country for which she was longing.

Herr Lindblad, who was in Paris at this time, wrote to his wife: "Jenny has engaged herself at too small a salary. This she now regrets, but it cannot now be helped. Her love for Sweden and the kind letter of the directors has dimmed her vision." And he tells of having taken Meyerbeer to see Jenny, who sang to him airs from *Roberto*, *Norma*, and several of Lindblad's own songs. Meyerbeer thought much of her voice, and wished to hear it in the Opera House, as he believed its carrying powers would be increased in a large space. This hearing actually did take place, and though through nervousness Mlle. Lind once more did herself no justice, Meyerbeer was so satisfied that he desired to engage her to create the chief part in an opera which he was writing for the opening of the new Berlin Opera House. He was of opinion that, even had her new contract with Stockholm not precluded her from accepting an engagement in Paris, she would find Berlin a far better European centre for the appreciation of her art, and the one she herself liked best.[1] Herr Lindblad wrote to his wife on July 25: "Jenny is now returning home, and longing for it with her whole heart after her year's exile. We shall be back by the 5th of August." And they were.

[1] It was not until many years later that a writer in the French newspaper *Ménéstrel* gave the facts as we give them, after it had been asserted that Mlle. Lind had sung, and failed in Paris.

CHAPTER III

1843–1844

MLLE. LIND'S reappearance in Stockholm, in the part of Norma was in marked contrast to her last performance of the part before she went to Paris, and it evoked immense enthusiasm. Her voice was now in its prime, and had acquired great sonority; it was capable of adapting itself to every shade of expression, and Mlle. Lind had now a technical command over it, great enough to be regarded as unique in the history of the musical world. The incredibly rapid development of Mlle. Lind's voice and technique during her visit to Paris made many people question the value of the instruction she had previously received, but such doubts must be dismissed as ungenerous. It must be remembered that before she went to seek Garcia's help she had been for many years a Theatre Scholar, and had to appear in public before her education was complete, a proceeding that did justice to neither pupil nor teacher, as well as being detrimental to the voice, The wonder is that the damage was not irrevocable.

During the nine months of her new engagement in Stockholm Mlle. Lind appeared 106 times in thirteen rôles. Five of them were new ones: Amazali in Spontini's *Ferdinand Cortez*, Valentine in *The Huguenots*, Minette in the *Gazza Ladra*, La Contessa in the *Nozze di Figaro*, and last but not least as Amina in the *Sonnambula*, one of her most famous representations. This she sang for the first time on March 1, 1843.

Besides her musical activities, this period was to see the final crisis in Mlle. Lind's home relations. These were still strained, and she had never gone back to live with her parents after her first stay with the Lindblads. Mlle. Lind now, out of her scanty earnings, bought a little house in the country, where she established her parents. But, as in those far-off days, by Swedish law, a woman if not under parental control had to have a legally appointed guardian until she married, Mlle. Lind had to gain her parents' consent to the appointment of one. She was fortunate in finding for this office a man of high character and wide sympathies, a good business man, and a keen lover of music. This was Judge Henrik Munthe, who managed not only her private business, but also, long after his guardianship ceased with her marriage, looked after the many charities and pensions with which Mlle. Lind endowed her countrymen and women.

A great event of this year (1843) was the National Jubilee to celebrate the twenty-fifth year of Carl Johann's reign. The royal family of the Bernadottes, in spite of their abrupt introduction to the country, had succeeded in gaining the support of the "National Association," and this celebration was to appeal to everything that was national and popular in Sweden.

Mlle. Lind took the part of a peasant girl from the Province of Wermland, in a divertissement produced by the Royal Theatre, and the performances ran through February and March into April. She was capitally supported by Signor Belletti in his own real character of an Italian, and Mlle. Lind put forth all the new powers she had gained in Paris.

We find the Court taking pleasure in showing her favour and friendship, and one of the ladies-in-waiting, Mlle. de Stedingk, describes her in her diary as of "faultless behaviour and reputation; her manners are pleasing and modest; without being pretty, she has an expression of purity and genius," and this description might well serve for all her life, though, naturally, as years went by she became more assured in manner and decided in speech.

By this time her fame had spread beyond Sweden, and "the Nightingale" could no longer be caged in her northern home. Offers came from Denmark and Finland, and from still farther afield, where Meyerbeer was claiming her for the chief part in his new opera, *Das Feldlager in Schlesien.* But Mlle. Lind wished to try her wings first nearer home in Denmark, in concerts, not in opera.

During the summer of 1843 Mlle. Lind, Julius Günther, and Jacob Josephson were giving concerts in the Swedish provinces, sometimes together, sometimes separately. With Günther she had sung at the Opera and in concerts, long before her visit to Paris, and they had obviously been brought together so much as to foreshadow the engagement which eventually took place. Josephson was a newer acquaintance. Born in 1818, he was a composer whose songs are well known in Sweden. But at the time to which we are now referring he was at a critical point in his career, longing to go abroad for study, but without the means to do so. This was a situation which Mlle. Lind thoroughly understood, for it had been her own. We shall see how she dealt with it.

The provincial tour was extended to Finland, where she met with success and kindness, referred to when hearing of her death by the Finnish poet Topelius, who had known her in this year of which we are speaking. And then she went to Copenhagen for the second time to sing in concerts.

Previous mention has been made of M. Bournonville as having heard her in 1839 in Stockholm and been indignant at the pittance for which she was singing, and he, now that she was again visiting Copenhagen, begged her to sing in *Roberto*. She was to sing in Swedish, while the rest of the cast sang in Danish, and all were working for the success of the event ; all but the chief person, whose terror of any but the Swedish stage still obsessed her. Insomuch that M. Bournonville proposed to cancel all arrangements. Her pride asserted itself, however, and as he began to doubt, she waxed courageous, and the experiment ended in a complete success.

We take this as a landmark and the end of her refusals to appear out of Sweden in opera.

In Copenhagen Mlle. Lind enjoyed the friendship and admiration of many eminent men, such as the painters Melbye and Jensen, the poet Oehlenschlaeger, and the sculptor Thorvaldsen, and above all, Hans Andersen, who conceived for her a devotion which

Jenny Lind

Du sang — jeg hörte henrykt Sangerinden,
Og dog, mon vel din bedste Sang du faaer?
Man Kunstnerinden glemme kan for Qvinden,
Jeg synger ei — for stærkt mit Hjerte slaaer!

H. C. Andersen

Kjøb. 11 Sept. 1843.

FREE TRANSLATION

You sang—I listened, enchanted singer,
And yet *my* best song you will receive,
One forgets the artist for the woman;
I do not sing my heart beats too strong.

A TRIBUTE FROM HANS ANDERSEN.

had all the mixture of simplicity and childlike faith which was so characteristic of him. He was a very ugly man, and on one occasion of special insistence on his devotion Mlle. Lind was cruel enough to hand him a mirror; but without any effect on his attentions.

Mlle. Lind was the first artist whom the Copenhagen students had ever serenaded; when they had escorted her home, she sang to them from her balcony, and then hurried away to a dark corner to weep out her emotions, and vow to be more and more efficient in the future.

This is the special note of her character; each success, instead of satisfying her, only stimulated her to further effort.

From Copenhagen Mlle. Lind returned to Sweden for a continuation of her provincial concerts. At Westervik she found herself once more in the company of Günther and Josephson, who had waited for her there, after having given a successful soirée of their own. Günther returned to Stockholm, but Josephson joined Mlle. Lind and her companion, who were going to Upsala, where Mlle. Lind gave a concert on September 30. At this concert she sang airs from *Figaro*, *Norma*, *Roberto*, and *Niobe*. The next day she returned to Stockholm for a year's work at her old, small salary.

Between October, 1843, and July, 1844, Mlle. Lind appeared sixty-six times in sixteen different characters, six of them new ones.

Armide by Gluck was one of them, and of it she wrote, when sending tickets to Judge Munthe: "I trust that you will greatly enjoy the music, which is so grand that my smallness will appear in its true light. But I am so thrilled by the sublime spirit of the music that I am ready to risk my own personality."

Mlle. Lind was now setting about a plan to help Josephson to go abroad to study, and in order to raise the funds, with Günther's assistance, she gave a concert at Upsala on Whit-Monday. Its success was beyond all expectations, and enabled Josephson's dreams to come true, and he went to Italy to study. In later years he became one of Sweden's foremost song writers.

In March, 1844, King Carl Johann died, and the Royal Theatre was closed for national mourning. We hear about those days in the following letter from Mlle. Lind to Hans Andersen. She often addressed her men friends as "Brother," in the same way that she addressed older women friends as "Mother," as was customary in Germany and Sweden in those days.

STOCKHOLM, *March 19th*, 1844.

MY GOOD BROTHER

Mr. Bournonville mentioned in his last letter that you had been shedding tears because of my silence. This, naturally, I take to be nonsense, but, as my conscience does reproach me in regard to you, I hasten to recall myself to your memory and ask my friend and brother not to be angry with me, but rather to furnish me soon with a proof that I have not forfeited my right to his friendship and good will. A thousand thousand thanks for the pretty tales! I find them divinely beautiful, and believe them to be the grandest and loveliest that ever flowed from your pen. I hardly know to which I should concede the palm, but on reflection I think "The Ugly Duckling" the prettiest. Oh, what a glorious gift to be able to clothe in words one's most lofty thoughts; by means of a scrap of paper to make men see so clearly how the noblest often lie most hidden and covered over by wretchedness and rags, until the hour of transformation strikes, and shows the figure in a divine light. Thanks, from all my heart for this, as touching as it is instructive....

This country is now in mourning—peace to all those who are gone! After all one is happiest when once well out of the way. Our Theatre is closed now for about seven weeks and this is not pleasant, but meanwhile we are busy studying new things. I must tell you, my good brother, that I have here quite a cosy little home. Cheerful sunny rooms, a nightingale and a greenfinch; the latter, however, is greatly superior as an artist to his celebrated colleague, for whilst the former remains on his perch grumpy and moody, the other jumps about in his cage, looking so joyous and good-natured, as if, to begin with, he was not in the least jealous, but instead, supposes himself created merely for the purpose of cheering his silent friend! And then he sings a song, so high, so deep, so charming and sonorous, that I sit down beside him and mutely sing praises to Him whose "strength is made perfect in weakness."—My dear friend, I do feel so happy now, I seem to have come from a stormy sea into a peaceful cottage.

Farewell, God bless and protect my brother is the sincere wish of his Aff: Sister

JENNY.

This peace was, however, of short duration. Meyerbeer was clamouring for her in good earnest, and Berlin had begun to take note of this new singer and wanted to hear her.

The records of Meyerbeer's proposals are not forthcoming, but some time in the summer they took sufficient shape to decide her to go to Germany, three weeks after the last of her engagements when she had sung Fiorilla in the *Turco in Italia*.

True to her thoroughness of purpose, Mlle. Lind determined to make a quiet study of her new part, not in Berlin but in Dresden, whither she went, accompanied by "Tante Lona," and Meyerbeer came there to study and consult with her. She was induced to sing soon after her arrival at a party at

Herr Kaskel's, who was the Swedish consul in Dresden. She sang Swedish songs first, and then the "Niobe" air in her grand style, with cadences, and the enthusiasm of the audience provided a happy inauguration of her future successes in Germany. Her intended period of study was, however, quickly disturbed by a recall to Sweden for the coronation of King Oscar the First, for Mlle. Lind as Court singer had to take part in ten performances during the Court festivities.

CHAPTER IV

1844–1845

THE Swedes now appreciated their gifted countrywoman so highly that they tried to induce her to accept an eight years' engagement at a salary that was to continue for life, and her friends had considerable difficulty in preventing Mlle. Lind from giving way to her love for home, and her constitutional dislike of the unknown, by accepting, and thus depriving herself of the larger and more brilliant life that was to be hers.

Fortunately the wiser counsels prevailed, and as soon as possible after her last performance of *Norma* on October 9, 1844, she really started on her European career, leaving for Germany, with Louise Johannsen as her companion. They stayed in the Französischer Strasse, Berlin, and while preparing for her debut she lived very quietly, though enjoying much kindness from private friends, and Meyerbeer arranged for a private presentation to the royal family, who invited her to sing at Court.

It was on this occasion, at the party given by the Princess of Prussia (afterwards the Empress Augusta) that we have the amusing account given by the wife of the British Ambassador, Lady Westmorland, a lady well able to judge of music and the sister arts. She describes how, on entering the concert room, she saw a pale, plain-faced girl, badly dressed and looking like a shy schoolgirl, sitting by the piano. Madame Sontag was also there as a guest, and everyone began speculating as to whether Meyerbeer had been playing a practical joke when raving about the new singer he had discovered. His answer to Lady Westmorland's inquiry was, however, merely: "Attendez, Miladi."

When the time came for Mlle. Lind to sing, the effect on the company was marvellous and instantaneous. The lovely notes came ringing out, and her face became transfigured with the fire and dignity of her genius, and there was no more doubt as to the powers of the artist in the minds of those present.

Mlle. Lind's own account of the same party may be given as interesting. It was written to her guardian, Judge Munthe, in Sweden:

I have sung at Court and been so fortunate as to please greatly. This may sound conceited, but I do not mean it so. The Countess Rossi (Mme. Sontag) was present, and my modesty prevents me from telling you what she is reported to have said. I am meeting with extraordinary success everywhere, and going much into fashionable society, because this gives the first entrance into the world of Art. And—do you know—I am already known in Berlin, and people talk of me with interest, so lively and so flattering, that I begin to think I must be in Stockholm. Forgive me, Dear Mr. Munthe, for thus openly speaking of things as they occur. I promise not to become proud and conceited; only glad and happy when things go well.

These interesting recollections prove that even before her first public appearance Mlle. Lind had won the hearts of a brilliant circle of friends, many of whom remained in affectionate intercourse with her all her life.

At this period also an event took place which exercised a marked influence on the artistic side of her career, and this was the memorable meeting with Mendelssohn in the house of their mutual friend, Professor Wichmann, the sculptor. Let us use her own description in a letter home dated October 22:

Last night I was invited to a very pleasant and elegantly furnished house, where I saw and spoke to Mendelssohn-Bartholdy, and he was incredibly polite and friendly, and spoke of my "great talent." I was a little surprised, and asked him on what ground he spoke that way. "Well," he said, " for this reason, that all who have heard you are of one opinion only, and that is so rare a thing, that it is quite sufficient to prove to me what you are."

Though Meyerbeer had written the part of Vielka in *Das Feldlager in Schlesien* for Mlle. Lind, there had been so much delay about her arrival in Berlin that the part had been sent for study to Mlle. Tuczec, who now claimed the right of first performance, though she really was unsuited to the rôle. Mlle. Lind refused to encroach on any claimed rights, and preferred to make her debut in Berlin in her favourite rôle of Norma. This she did, after her usual period of nervous dread, on December 15, when she completely conquered her audience and disarmed the critics. The heroines of the past and present were forgotten, and Mlle. Lind's new and original rendering of the part commended itself to all.

The foremost critic of the day, Rellstab, who was a poet as well as a writer, and the author of the libretto of the *Feldlager* (" Camp of Silesia "), praised her performance in no measured tones, and later critics agreed that his praise and enthusiasm were not exaggerated.

Bellini originally wrote *Norma* for Mme. Pasta, in 1832, and the famous air " Casta diva " was sung by her in the key of G. Mlle. Lind was the first to sing it in the softer key of F, since generally adopted.

In *La Sonnambula* Mlle. Lind created so profound a sensation that the prices were raised, for the second performance, to a degree unprecedented in the German theatrical world, and the critics proclaimed her as having raised the art of singing to glorious heights.

From the day of her debut Mlle. Lind was accepted in Berlin as of supreme attainments, and she rescued Meyerbeer's *Feldlager in Schlesien* from the failure that threatened it, owing to Mlle. Tuczec's rendering of an unsuitable part.

Besides the Meyerbeer opera Mlle. Lind sang frequently in *La Sonnambula* and *Norma*, but she did not wish to sing in the *Freischütz* till she was more sure of her German. Weber's *Euryanthe* had been revived at a performance in aid of a monument to be erected to his memory in Dresden, after the removal, by a few of his admirers, of his remains from London, where he had died. But even Mlle. Lind could not rouse much enthusiasm for the opera, though the critics pronounced her reading as being nearer the composer's intentions than previous attempts had been.

Meanwhile London was getting interested in Berlin's enthusiasm for this new Swedish singer, and

Mr. Bunn, the lessee of Drury Lane Theatre, arrived and caught the diva in an unwary moment. Amid the excitement of a performance as Vielka, in an *entr'acte* Mlle. Lind was invited to the British Ambassador's (Lord Westmorland) box, where she found Mr. Bunn. In the glamour of such security and, without any time to consider, she was led to sign a contract of which she repented forthwith. Her perplexities and heart-searchings preyed upon her mind so much that she fell ill, though no one really knew the true cause. Meyerbeer, like other friends, must have thought nervousness the cause, for he wrote her the letter (reproduced on pp. 38, 39), when he called in vain to see her. The translation is as follows:

BERLIN, *Feb.* 28, 1845.

MY DEAR MADEMOISELLE,

Though I have called on you several times since your indisposition, I have not been so fortunate as some of your other friends in seeing you.

It only therefore remains, for me to express in writing my congratulations and good wishes on the anniversary of your fête which I understand occurs to-day, and to beg you, at the same time kindly to accept these few flowers, modest and pure as yourself.

But what remains for your friends to wish, for you whom Heaven has so richly endowed! It has given you that great

Ma chère Mademoiselle!

Quoique je me sois présenté plusieurs fois chez Vous depuis votre indisposition, je n'ai jamais pu être aussi heureux que plusieurs autres de Vos Amis de Vous voir. Il ne me reste donc qu'à Vous exprimer par écrit mes congratulations & mes voeux pour l'anniversaire de votre fête qui, comme m'a dit Madame Reier, a lieu aujourd'hui, & de Vous prier en même temps, de vouloir bien agréer ces quelques fleurs, modestes & pures comme Vous même.

Mais que reste-t-il à Vos amis de souhaiter aujourd'hui pour Vous, que le ciel a si richement douée? Il Vous a donné cette voix suave et sympathique qui charme & émeut les coeurs; la flamme du génie qui pénètre votre chant & votre jeu; et enfin ces graces indécibles que la modestie, la candeur & l'innocence, donnent seules à leurs élus, & qui subjugent jusqu'aux ennemis. —— On ne pourroit donc demander pour Vous au ciel tout au plus, que de Vous ôter ces doutes dans la puissance de votre Talent, qui font des jours d'angoisse de vos jours de triomphe;

de Vous oter encore cette indécision & ~~cette~~ irrésolution, qui Vous jette dans de continuelles agitations, & enfin de faire disparaitre cette humeur soupçonneuse, qui Vous rendant défiante de la source des Sympathies que Vous inspirez, pourrait peut-être à la fin Vous priver de la plus belle consolation de la vie humaine, de l'amitié. —— Mais que le ciel Vous accorde ou non ce petit supplément à vos autres qualités précieuses, toujours ma chère Mademoiselle, êtes Vous pour moi une des plus touchantes & nobles apparitions que j'ai rencontré dans mes longues peregrinations artistiques, & à laquelle j'ai voué pour toute la vie, l'admiration & l'estime la plus sincère & la plus profonde. Votre

28 Fevrier 45.

tout devoué
Meyerbeer

D

and sympathetic voice which charms and moves all hearts; the fire of genius which pervades your singing and your acting; and in fine, those indelible graces which modesty, candour, and innocence give only to the favoured few and which bring every enemy into subjection.

One can, therefore, ask nothing more for you from Heaven, than relief from those doubts in the power of your talent which turn even your days of triumph into days of anxiety; the removal of that indecision and irresolution which throw you into such continual agitation; and finally, the disappearance of that diffident temperament, which, rendering you distrustful of the source of the sympathies you inspire, may, perhaps in the end, deprive you of the most beautiful consolation of human life, friendship.

But whether Heaven grants you or not, this little supplement to your other precious qualities, you will always be for me, my dear Mademoiselle, one of the most touching and noble characters that I have met during my long artistic wanderings, and one to whom I have vowed for my whole life the most profound and sincere admiration and esteem.

Ever your devoted

MEYERBEER.

One cannot help thinking that this full if friendly criticism made an impression on the recipient, for we find Mlle. Lind hesitating no more, but deciding to take her benefit in *Norma* on March 11 rather than in the *Freischütz* in German, of which she then really did not know enough.

Before closing her first Berlin season Mlle. Lind sang at a Court concert and two public ones. The last of these took place as her "Farewell" at the Sing-Akademie and was in aid of the asylum for blind soldiers. At all these concerts there was nothing but enthusiasm and praise, none of which altered the singer's modest and simple demeanour.

A description of her at that time by Josephson was not far wrong, which said that "she was wavering between heaven and earth, not knowing on what terms she was with either."

On leaving Berlin at the end of her season Mlle. Lind made her first appearance at Hanover and sang several of her favourite rôles to a friendly public. She also sang at Court, where she became a great favourite with the Crown Prince and Princess, who continued their friendship when they succeeded to the throne. She then visited various towns in Germany before reaching Hamburg *en route* for Stockholm, where already a playbill on the doors of the Royal Theatre announced the return of the favourite. She had left Stockholm the idol of Sweden, she returned the idol of Northern Europe. It was the old, old story; wildest excitement on one side, feverish yearning for retirement on the other; the wanderer wanted the peace of a home not the shouts of the multitude.

Mlle. Lind now sang at the Opera eighteen times, eight times in *La Figlia del Reggimento*, which rôle always had a special charm for her, who loved military music. One performance was given entirely for soldiers, invited by the King, and the little *vivandière* was as delighted with her audience as they were with her.

With the prospect of a holiday, she went to stay with friends in the country, but it was to be of short duration. The King of Prussia was going to entertain Queen Victoria and the Prince Consort at two of his castles on the Rhine. The occasion was interesting as being the first visit from the Queen of England since her accession to the throne and marriage, and it was to coincide with the inauguration of a statue to Beethoven at Bonn. A galaxy of royalties and music-lovers from every European country was to gather together and Mlle. Lind was invited to sing privately to King Frederick William and his guests, both at the Castle of Brühl and at the newly restored Castle of Stolzenfels. The newspapers could give no account of these private doings, but we are indebted to the private journal kept by Mrs. George Grote, the wife of the historian, for an account of this, as of many other events of Mlle. Lind's life in those busy and interesting years.

Though Mrs. Grote was not herself present at the royal gathering she knew many people who were, and from them, as well as from Mlle. Lind later, she was aware of the events and of the impressions made by them.

Mrs. Grote reported as to the high expectations as to Mlle. Lind's gifts which the German praises had raised in the minds of the illustrious gathering, and how some people were prepared for disillusionment.

King Leopold, who had already heard Mlle. Lind in Berlin and was aware of the scepticism in the air, smilingly silenced the doubters, saying, "You will be satisfied; she is quite extraordinary," and he amused himself by watching the effect her first air produced on the listeners, as of the sun piercing through a fog; till everyone basked in the sunshine.

The Queen and Prince Albert were both delighted with the treat provided for them, and expressed the hope that the singer would soon visit England. One of the doubters surrendered to King Leopold when he said, "The combination of style, vocal skill, and quality of voice takes one by storm." Mlle. Lind also sang at the second castle and captivated the whole courtly circle by her manners as well as by her music.

At the end of the festivities Mlle. Lind was engaged to visit Frankfort, where the utmost impatience was felt to see and judge one who was making such a sensation in the musical world. The engagement was for nine nights, and included performances of *Norma*, *Der Freischütz*, and *Lucia*.

Here, at Frankfort, it was that Mlle. Lind actually first met Mr. and Mrs. George Grote, of whom she had heard much through her friends in Sweden, Madame von Koch and Mr. Edward Lewin, whose sister Mrs. Grote was. With the feeling of confidence with which her new friends inspired her, Mlle. Lind told them of the nightmare from which she was suffering over the Bunn contract. Mrs. Grote, with her knowledge of the world, became of great help to Mlle. Lind when she eventually did reach London, and she stayed in her house in Eccleston Street while Clairville Cottage was being prepared by Mr. Lumley, and also frequently visited the Grotes at their country house at Burnham Beeches.

It was at about this time that a proposal was sent to Mlle. Lind from Herr Pokorny, the lessee of the famous Opera House in Vienna, to appear there in the following winter, for five performances. It was a great opportunity, but the usual heart-searchings and terrible nervousness supervened. To one of her great friends she wrote:

Everything goes well with me, and yet I have such

SCENE IN THE 2ND ACT OF "LA FIGLIA DEL REGGIMENTO."

From a water-colour drawing by Edouard Lehmann, made at Copenhagen, 1845

anxiety about Vienna, that I hardly think I dare go. They have such excellent singers there, and if I do not please, I shall lose my whole reputation.

And she would give no answer, but went to her many friends in Copenhagen. There she sang in *Norma* and the *Figlia*, and on October 10 (1845) she sang at the Court Theatre of the Palace of Christiansborg in aid of the Association for the Rescue of Neglected Children, a cause that always appealed to her, and for which she sang in other countries as well. On this visit she renewed acquaintance with the sculptor Thorvaldsen, as also with Hans Andersen, on whom she made the lasting impression that is shown in some of his writings. The weather was very bad, and she caught a severe cold, which threatened her with loss of voice, so that she had to cancel several German engagements.

The Bunn affair was worrying her, as he had written to say that she must appear at Drury Lane on October 19. The contract was not really valid owing to Bunn not having signed his name on the counterpart. In her inexperience, however, Mlle. Lind had written an unfortunate letter, in which, instead of pointing out this invalidity, she asked him, "as a favour," to cancel the contract, which of course he would not do. Whereof more hereafter.

CHAPTER V

1845–1846

WITH the approach of winter we find Mlle. Lind once more on her way to Berlin, where she had accepted an invitation to stay in the house of Professor and Mme. Wichmann. It was for these friends that she commissioned the painter Magnus to paint the portrait of her which has become so well known. Magnus painted a replica of the picture, which Mlle. Lind retained and which is still in her family. The Wichmann portrait is now in the National Portrait Gallery in Berlin ; much prized, both for its subject and as being a fine example of a favourite German painter's work. Magnus at the same time painted a portrait of Mendelssohn for Mlle. Lind which at her death was bequeathed to Mendelssohn's elder daughter, Mrs. Victor Benecke.

The Magnus portrait is the most widely known, but innumerable others were painted, both with and without sittings. There are two famous examples in Stockholm, one by Asher, a German painter, where

JENNY LIND.
From the Painting by Eduard Magnus.

she is seated at the piano with a lace shawl over her shoulders (now used as a bridal veil in her family), and another by Södermark, in the costume of Norma. This picture was subscribed for by the employees of the Royal Opera House in Stockholm and was hung there, in 1849. There is also a beautiful marble bust in that foyer by Christian Erichsen, and one by Joseph Durham used similarly to stand in Her Majesty's Theatre in London before the old house was burnt down. There are also many Baxter colour prints, and a few of the old pottery representations of those days survive.

Count D'Orsay, the well-known dandy of early-Victorian days, also painted Mlle. Lind in the costume of Norma, when he had taken to portrait painting for an income, but it is more an object of interest than a work of art.

The Berlin season of 1845–1846 was a brilliant one, during which Mlle. Lind sang twenty-eight times, including a benefit night. As her second, like her first season, was only for *Gastrollen*—what we should call " star parts "—there exist no contracts to show the fees she received, and throughout her career it is difficult to find records for any concert that she did not give herself, in Europe ; and at many of these she gave the entire proceeds to charity.

Mlle. Lind appeared for the first time on November 19, 1845, as Donna Anna in Mozart's *Don Giovanni*, Mlle. Tuczec winning high praise as Zerlina. The performance was so fine that it was repeated five times during the season with increasing interest and raised prices.

Then came her first appearance in Berlin in the eminently German opera, Weber's *Freischütz*, in which work she had made her first memorable debut as Agathe, when eighteen years of age. Herr Rellstab struck the right note when, in analysing her performance, he pointed out her love for the masterpiece as a whole; for she played the rôle of the maiden who was the child of Nature, as she herself was, without any thought of the prima donna who was singing her favourite airs; and this reading called forth true recognition of the simplicity which high art can attain.

In view of the frequent mention of her nervousness and indecision it is a curious fact that Mlle. Lind yet received the enthusiastic applause lavished on her with great calm. But it would be a great mistake to infer that she was either insensible to, or ungrateful for, the admiration which she excited. The secret of her calm was that she accepted it, not for herself, but on behalf of the Art of Music of which she was the most ardent worshipper in the throng. This attitude is shown by a letter to her friend and teacher, Mme. Erichsen, dated Berlin, November 24, 1845:

It was with the wildest pleasure that I had the honour to receive your kind letter and I cannot thank you enough for it. I use no empty words when I say that my rejoicing was intense, for I cannot forget that it was you who guided my sensitive young mind first towards high aims, or that it was you who saw beneath the surface and fancied you saw something behind those insignificant grey eyes of mine. How changed everything is now! All the musical talent of Europe is, so to speak at my feet! What great things the Almighty has vouchsafed to me! The Berlin public is terribly critical, but I like this, for if I take pains I am at least properly appreciated. They want to analyse my every gesture, every shade of expression. Indeed one has to be careful, but it all tends to mental cultivation. I have to bear no trifling comparisons, for the moment I step forward I am measured with the Sontag measure, or that of the greatest artists that Germany has produced. Perhaps you think I have grown vain? God forbid, and shield me from that. I know what I can do and what I can not. I have not quite made up my mind whether I will go to Vienna in the spring. Meanwhile I wonder if I may tell you, that next autumn I mean to return home and settle down quietly, caring nothing for the world. You will call this a crime. But please reflect, just a little, how difficult it is to stand all this racing about, alone! alone! having to rely on my own judgment for everything and yet so absorbed in my rôles. Oh, it is not easy. However we will talk no more about this now. Enough to say that the Stage has no attraction for me; my soul is yearning for rest from all these compliments and adulation.

I am your grateful pupil,

JENNY LIND.

It is rather amusing in the beginning of this letter to find the criticized in the rôle of critic, and the end of the letter quite tallies with what Mlle. Lind had said to Mrs. Grote at their Frankfort meeting a couple of months before.

In another letter of the same date to Mr. Josephson, who was studying in Italy, she tells how she is enjoying Berlin, andt hat her voice has grown twice as strong as it used to be, her middle register being now quite clear. She would so like to go to Italy, but must first earn some money, and may have to go to Vienna in the spring for that purpose. This is a characteristic instance of Mlle. Lind's almost quixotic generosity; having given someone else the means to do what she denied herself.

Since Mlle. Lind's first meeting with Mendelssohn their friendship had become a firm and inspiring one. They met whenever he came to Berlin, but his home was in Leipzig, where he conducted the famous *Gewandhaus* concerts, acknowledged to be the finest concerts in Europe in those days. Mendelssohn was anxious that Mlle. Lind should sing under his bâton at one of these concerts, and evidently the Berlin director gave leave of absence without difficulty, for the day after Mlle. Lind's second performance in the *Freischütz* she travelled to Leipzig and stayed in the house of Mme. Frederick Brockhaus, a sister of Richard Wagner.

Though the price of tickets was doubled, the rush for their possession would have filled the hall four times over, and the students of the Conservatoire had their prescriptive right of admission denied them. In view of subsequent events it is interesting to know that at an indignation meeting of the students, the one of their number chosen to call with a protest on the directors was Otto Goldschmidt. He, subsequently, was fortunate enough to obtain a ticket for himself by purchase.

Mlle. Lind captured even this critical audience from her first note in a *Norma* air, through a duet from *Romeo and Juliet* with Miss Dolby, to the enthusiasm of her songs by Mendelssohn, accompanied by him, and her final favourite Swedish songs.

At a second concert, in aid of the fund for the widows of the *Gewandhaus* Orchestra, she received a wonderful ovation of thanks, to which she made Mendelssohn respond, standing by his side on the balcony of the house where she was staying.

The following day Mlle. Lind returned to Berlin to appear in *Don Giovanni* and to carry on engagements of which an important one was Julia in Spontini's *Vestale*. Mlle. Lind had previously only sung the rôle six times in Stockholm, where the opera was not suited to Swedish tastes. But in Berlin it had long been a favourite work, originally staged under the composer's personal direction, and Mlle. Lind once again challenged previous readings of the part. At first her admirer Rellstab was disappointed in the effect she produced in the first act, but in the end he recognized the perfection of the climax, to which, with her unerring instinct, she sacrificed those minor effects which secure a passing triumph at the expense of logic and coherence. Mlle. Lind invariably kept her dramatic power in reserve, with a reticence which only great artists are known to exercise, till the moment when dramatic truth requires its fulfilment.

Enough is known of Rellstab's character and position in Berlin as a critic to establish the certainty that he honestly meant every word he wrote in praise of Mlle. Lind, though nowadays he might seem guilty of exaggeration.

To this period would seem to belong a charming letter from Mendelssohn which speaks for itself in the accompanying reproduction.

Leipzig d 23 December
1845

Mein liebes Fräulein

Für Ihren lieben, guten, freundlichen Brief möchte ich Ihnen so gern danken, möchte Ihnen sagen welche Freude Sie mir dadurch bereitet haben — durch den Brief, und durch das Andenken, das Sie mir erhalten haben! Aber Sie wissen es ja, welche Freude Sie mir dadurch machen; und der Dank spricht sich doch niemals durch Worte aus; gerade wo man am besten sagen möchte, da geht's am wenigsten. Ihr Brief erinnert mich oft an Lindblad; der hatte auch die deutsche Grammatik nicht gelernt, und schrieb besser und inniglicher, als es die meisten Deutschen können; ich habe manche Stelle aus seinen Briefen mein Lebelang nicht vergessen, und so ist es bei Ihnen auch. Wie sagte die Königin von Preußen? Verwundern Sie sich nur nicht. Ich glaube, ich hätte das erfunden, wenn sie es nicht vorher gesagt hätte; und so oft ich Ihren Brief gelesen habe, und so oft ich an Sie denke komme ich darauf immer wieder zurück.

Morgen ist nun Weihnachtsabend, und seit Sie von Leipzig fort sind hatte ich den Wunsch an den Abend

auch unter denen sein zu dürfen, die Ihnen eine Gabe bringen
konnten ~~Ihre~~ viele sein; aber aufrichtiger und herzlicher
kann es keiner mit Ihnen meinen, als ich. Darum bitte
ich Sie, nehmen Sie die Lieder an. Jetzt ist mir's eigentlich
ganz so, als müßte ich etwas Anderes sagen, daß ich die
Zahl der Lieder-Componisten vermehre, die sich zu Ihnen
drängen — aber ich sehe mir das abgerechnet, und bedenke, daß
Sie es schon einmal „mal placé" gefunden haben. Worüber
ich mich aber in jedem Falle entschuldigen sollte, das sind
die Zueignungen — aber an denen ist wieder blos das Hof-
Concert (Schuld) und das Compliment das wir da über mein Zuhören
gemacht wurden. Als Sie sagten, Sie könnten auch bringen; da
nahm ich mir gleich vor, ~~[illegible]~~ einmal etwas für Sie zu zueignen, so
gut (schlecht) ich's eben könnte. Doch ist's diesmal durch
viele Störungen so weniger gut geworden, als ich hoffte — nehmen
Sie's so vorlieb; wenigstens fehlen die „rosen och de bladen"
und die „goldenen Streuälein" und das schwedische Brod nicht.

Für das schwedische Brod möchte ich noch einmal ganz
besonders danken. Bitte, mein liebes Fräulein, schneiden Sie
auch manchmal selbst ein Brod, und vergessen Sie es nicht, solange

Sie in Berlin sind; das ist eine solche Freude, die wir alle davon haben; denn wir essen da alle sehr gerne, d. die Kinder juchzen immer so, wenn wir ein Brod „von der Fräulein Lind" gekommen ist, und ich dachte, daß Sie „Augustern" zu uns geschickt haben. Als es neulich kam, da hatten die Kinder am Morgens auf der Straße Ihr Portrait hängen sehen, und waren plötzlich alle hingelaufen, und riefen: da wären Sie. Ich fragte ob sie den Namen hätten lesen können, sie sagten „nein, sie hätten's erkannt, aber es sei nicht ähnlich." Ich wollte dabei eine lehrreiche Bemerkung machen, daß es doch ähnlich sein müßte, aber es fiel mir ein, daß mirs auch so damit geht. Und als wir zu Hause kamen, da kam das Brod, und Abends kam Ihr Brief.

Das war ein schöner Tag, mein liebes Fräulein, und ich werd ihn niemals vergessen. Und nun muß ich den Brief schließen, weil die Post geht, die ihn morgen zu Ihnen bringen soll. Wenn wir in Schweden, so würfe ich das Paket in Ihre Thüre hinein (nicht wahr?), wär ich in Berlin so brächte ich Ihnen, und das thäte ich am liebsten Es bringt es der Briefträger und ich bitte Sie gütigst Sie

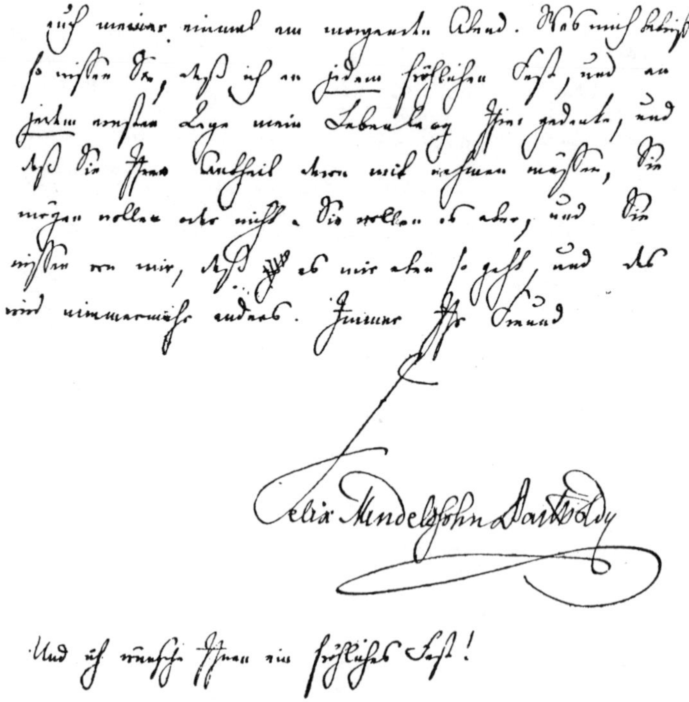

auch meiner einmal am morgenden Abend. Was mich betrifft so wissen Sie, daß ich an jedem fröhlichen Fest, und an jedem ernsten Tage mein Lebenlang Ihrer gedenke, und daß Sie Ihren Antheil daran mit nehmen müssen, Sie mögen wollen oder nicht. Sie wollen es aber, und Sie wissen von mir, daß es mir eben so geht, und das wird nimmermehr anders. Immer Ihr Freund

Felix Mendelssohn Bartholdy

Und ich wünsche Ihnen ein fröhliches Fest!

The translation is as follows:

LEIPZIG, 23*rd Dec.*, 1845.

MY DEAR FRÄULEIN,

For your dear, kind, friendly, letter I would so much like to thank you, and say how much pleasure you have given me with the letter and its kind thought of me. You know of course what pleasure you give me by remembering me, and yet, gratitude is never expressed in words,—just when one would like to be fluent, one never succeeds. Your

MENDELSSOHN ALBUM.

These decorations were made by Mendelssohn himself, in pencil and water-colour, on the cover of his album of MS. songs.

letter reminds me of Lindblad; he also had never mastered German grammar, and yet wrote better and more fervently [*innerlich*] than most Germans can. I have remembered some of the passages in his letters all my life, and I can say the same of yours. You remember what the Queen of Prussia said to you: " Verändern Sie Sich nur nicht " [only don't change]—I think I should have invented that remark if she had not said it first, and as often as I have read your letters, and as often as I think of you, I always come back to those words.

To-morrow is Christmas Eve, and ever since you left Leipzig, I have wished for permission to be among those who bring you gifts. There will be many to do so, but none heartier or more sincere than I, and so I beg you to accept these songs. I now feel that I want to say something about increasing the number of song-composers who crowd round you—but I have taught myself to refrain, as I think you would find it " malplacé."—But above all I must apologize for the drawings but the fault lies with the compliments I received at the Court Concert—When you said that you too could dance, I determined to do some drawings for you as well (badly) as I could. This time, however, many interruptions have made them less good than I hoped, Please forgive; at least I have not omitted the " rosen och de bladen " (Swedish) and the gold stars, and the Swedish bread.

I would again specially thank you for the Swedish bread. Please Dear Fräulein, send us sometimes such a loaf, and don't forget it as long as you are in Berlin; we all enjoy it so much, and eat it with so much pleasure; and the children jump for joy when a loaf comes from Fräulein Lind, and I thank you for sending one yesterday. The other day the children saw your portrait in the street, and they ran to it and said it was you, and when I asked them if they had read your name, they said, " No, they recognized you but the portrait was not like you." I wanted to make an instructive remark, that it must have been like, for them to have recognized it, but I left it alone.—And when we got home, there was your bread, and in the evening, there was your letter.—That was a very happy day, my Dear Fräulein, and I shall not forget it. And now I must close my letter, as the post is going, which will bring it to you to-morrow. If we were in Sweden, I should throw the packet in at your door (should I not?) If I were in Berlin I should take it to you,—and that is what I would soonest do—as it is, the postman will take it, and I beg of you to think of me to-morrow evening.

As far as I am concerned, you know that at *every* happy Festival and on *every* serious day, I think of you, and you have a share in them, whether you like it or no——But you wish it, I am sure, and you know from me that it is the same with me and never will be otherwise.

Always your friend
FELIX MENDELSSOHN BARTHOLDY.

And I wish you a Happy Christmas!

The songs contained in the album referred to in this letter are *Schilflied*, *Frühlingslied*, *Tröstung*, *Fahrwohl*, *Abendlied*, and *Ein altes Lied*. They are all dated Christmas, 1845, except the *Ein, noch viel alteres Lied* (words by Klingemann), which is dated "Aachen, June, 1846."* Because these songs were written out for Mlle. Lind it does not mean that they were new at the time or were dedicated to her.

These allusions to Swedish customs, and the use of Swedish words, often occurred in Mendelssohn's letters to Mlle. Lind, for before he knew her he had met the Swedish song-writer Lindblad, who has already been mentioned as a prop and stay to Mlle. Lind in her young days. The reproduction of the sketch, facing p. 56, shows the Christmas-tree on the billiard-table of the Wichmanns' house, and the train probably is in allusion to her many journeys.

To all Germans and Scandinavians Christmas was a day of great importance, long before the Christmas-tree and its candles became acclimatized in England, and to the end of her life Mme. Goldschmidt retained her old feelings about the celebration. Not only as a time of Church celebration and feasting, but as a time of good-will and giving help and pleasure to others.

We already may anticipate the Christmas at Havana when Mlle. Lind had a joke on Mr. Barnum; in like manner she would prepare her presents for weeks in advance, according to the known wants and tastes

* It was written in at the Aachen Festival.

of the lucky recipients. After she married and had a household, when her tree was lit, Mme. Goldschmidt, her friends and children would gather round the little Müller harmonium given her in 1849 by Salis Schwabe, and sing "Good King Wenceslas" and many other less well-known carols to her own accompaniment and leadership.

We must beg our readers to forgive this digression on the subject of Christmas, and return with us to Berlin at the date of Mlle. Lind's last twenty-six performances there, which included a first appearance as Valentine in *Les Huguenots*. She closed with a benefit night, and the house was crowded from floor to ceiling. The audience refused to disperse without some spoken words from the singer; dumb bows and thanks not being enough. Not yet being fluent in German, she contented herself and the audience with the few but sincere words, "I thank you, and will never forget this moment."

Thus on April 2, 1846, Mlle. Lind's second season ended in Berlin with mutual good-will, and she turned her thoughts to the engagement which she had at last made to go to Vienna. She spent a few days at Leipzig again, singing on April 12 at a *Gewandhaus* concert, to Mendelssohn's accompaniment, and this was the occasion of her first meeting

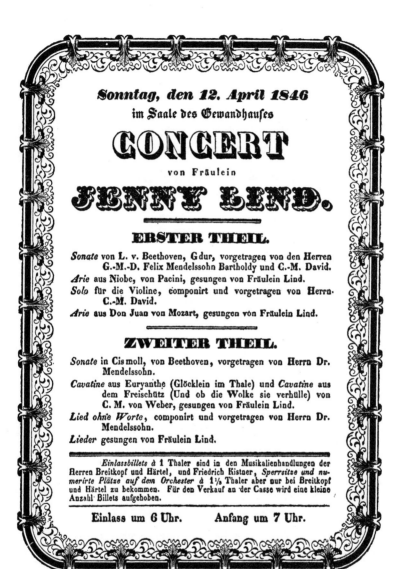

Sonntag, den 12. April 1846

im Saale des Gewandhauses

CONCERT

von Fräulein

JENNY LIND.

ERSTER THEIL.

Sonate von L. v. Beethoven, Gdur, vorgetragen von den Herren G.-M.-D. Felix Mendelssohn Bartholdy und C.-M. David.

Arie aus Niobe, von Pacini, gesungen von Fräulein Lind.

Solo für die Violine, componirt und vorgetragen von Herrn C.-M. David.

Arie aus Don Juan von Mozart, gesungen von Fräulein Lind.

ZWEITER THEIL.

Sonate in Cis moll, von Beethoven, vorgetragen von Herrn Dr. Mendelssohn.

Cavatine aus Euryanthe (Glöcklein im Thale) und *Cavatine* aus dem Freischütz (Und ob die Wolke sie verhülle) von C. M. von Weber, gesungen von Fräulein Lind.

Lied ohne Worte, componirt und vorgetragen von Herrn Dr. Mendelssohn.

Lieder gesungen von Fräulein Lind.

Einlassbillets à 1 Thaler sind in den Musikalienhandlungen der Herren Breitkopf und Härtel, und Friedrich Kistner, *Sperrsitze und numerirte Plätze auf dem Orchester à* 1⅓ Thaler aber nur bei Breitkopf und Härtel zu bekommen. Für den Verkauf an der Casse wird eine kleine Anzahl Billets aufgehoben.

Einlass um 6 Uhr. Anfang um 7 Uhr.

Programme of the Concert at Leipzig, April 12, 1846

with Mme. Schumann, who had come over from Dresden where she was living, intending only to take a seat in the audience. There was no orchestra for this concert, and Mendelssohn had undertaken to "preside at the piano" as well as to play some *Lieder ohne Worte* and the Moonlight Sonata. Though unprepared, even with a suitable concert garment, Mme. Schumann consented to replace Mendelssohn in some of his soli, and she was rapturously received when she played his *Lieder* and a *Scherzo* of her own.

The happy audience little thought that this was the last time Mendelssohn would play to them, though he conducted one more orchestral *Gewandhaus* concert before his death in the following year.

Madame Mendelssohn was a charming Frenchwoman whose family was domiciled in Frankfort, where Mendelssohn met her. She was ten years younger than her husband when they married in 1837, and Mendelssohn was devoted to her and their children.

As in Berlin with the Wichmanns, where Mlle. Lind stayed so much, the Mendelssohns' happy family life touched a deep note in her nature, which showed itself in a certain wistfulness in her letters of those days. Madame Mendelssohn only survived her husband six years.

CHAPTER VI

1846–1847

VIA Carlsbad and Prague, with a few days spent in each place, Mlle. Lind arrived in Vienna and took up her quarters at the house of Dr. Vivanot. Count Pokorny had engaged her for five performances at the then generous terms of £50 a performance with an extra benefit. At the time of which we are writing (1846) the Opera House was the largest theatre, as well as the handsomest, in Vienna. It seemed so large to the timid artist when she attended her first *Norma* rehearsal that she felt convinced her voice would never fill it, and she suffered terrors which were quite uncalled for. Mlle. Lind's voice was of a quality to fill the largest theatre ever built in Europe, and the Vienna house was far from being that.

The scene at her debut in *Norma* was a repetition of what had taken place in Berlin, and the effect on the audience was instantaneous and enthusiastic, though the inefficiency of the support rendered her by the chorus, orchestra, and even soloists was sharply criticized. It is true that there was a strong party against Mlle. Lind in Vienna ; a clique which had tried to prevent her coming to Vienna at all. But she triumphed over all difficulties, and in her *Sonnambula* moved the coldest and most prejudiced hearers, by her union of the purest vocal methods with touching and sincere playing of the part.

As we have quoted the Berlin critics we may as well give some words of the editor of the *Wiener Allgemeine Musik Zeitung*, a journal by no means predisposed to praise Mlle. Lind. After saying in one part of his paper: " For the initiated in music—those who listen, not with the ear only, but with the soul and the spirit—the appearance of Jenny Lind is an event altogether exceptional; such as has never before been witnessed, and will probably never be repeated," he sums up his criticism of Norma with the words:

The appearance of Mlle. Lind is of the deepest significance in all its aspects, and her achievements in Art deserve in the highest degree, the universal acknowledgment that they have received. She is the perfect picture of noblest womanhood and has, through her artistic aims, and the high perfection of her artistic cultivation, united to her great and many-sided talents, already won the sympathy of the entire public on her first appearance, in a way that few singers have ever won it before her. I count the moments that passed at her debut among the most enjoyable artistic pleasures that I have ever experienced, and eagerly look forward to her forthcoming performances.

During this period in Vienna, letters were passing between Mendelssohn, Mlle. Lind, and Mme. Birch-Pfeiffer, as to an opera which the composer wished to write for the singer. Mme. Birch-Pfeiffer was a German authoress of repute, who had coached Mlle. Lind in her German studies, before and after her first appearance in Berlin, and the two ladies kept up a voluminous correspondence. After her debut Mlle. Lind wrote to her friend and teacher:

WIEN, 23 *April*, 1846.

DEAR FRIEND,

It is over, at last—thank God, and I hasten to describe it to you, though I know that the kind-hearted Director, Pokorny has written all about it to you, to-day. Well then! Yesterday was the all-important day on which I appeared in *Norma*, and the good God did not desert me, though I deserved it for my unreasonable nervousness. Do not be angry with me, I beg you! I can do nothing with regard to that, and suffer enough for it, myself. The three days beforehand were dreadful. The idea was ever in my mind of turning back, but I should have given offence to so many if I had done so.

But now we shall be jolly here for a little while, and sing nine times; and then we can go on still farther.

But this Public! At the close I was called back sixteen times and twelve or fourteen before that. Just count that up! And the reception! I was quite astounded!

How are you all? A raging headache prevents me from writing more. I have not yet calmed down since yesterday.

Your truly loving JENNY.

Mlle. Lind had evidently written a similar account to Mendelssohn, and we will give a few paragraphs from his long letter of reply:

LEIPZIG, *May* 7, 1846.

MY DEAR FRÄULEIN

You are indeed a good and excellent Fräulein Lind. That is what I wanted to say to you (and I have said it often enough in thought) after receiving your first letter from Vienna written so soon after your opening performance.

That you wrote to me on the very next day; that you knew there was no one to whom it would give greater pleasure than to myself; and that you found time for it, and let nothing hinder you, or hold you back—all this was too good and kind of you!

Your description of the first evening, and of the twenty-five times you were called before the curtain, etc., etc., reminded me of an old letter written to me by my sister, when I was in London, a long time ago, and I looked for the old letter till I found it.

It was the first time that I had left the shelter of the parental roof, or had produced anything in public; and it had gone well, and a stone had been lifted from my heart, and I had written an account of it all to her. And thereupon she answered me thus:—There was nothing new to her, she said, in all that, for she had known it all quite certainly beforehand; she could not therefore clearly explain to herself why, in spite of this it had been so pleasant to her to hear it all confirmed; it was very pleasant, all the same.

It is precisely so with me, when I received your letter. And then, you write so well! In fact, when I get a letter from you it is exactly as if I saw you or heard you speak. I can see the expression of your face at every word that stands written before me, and I understand all that took place on the first *Norma* evening at Vienna almost as well as if I had been there. . . .

I really feel, however more pleasure in the enthusiasm of the Viennese, and the twenty-five calls before the curtain, than these few lines will express to you. It is great fun for me too, not because of what people call triumph, or success or anything of that kind, but because of the succession of pleasant days and evenings that it expresses, and the numbers of delighted and friendly faces with which you are surrounded. You must tell me all about this very particularly; or rather I must worm it out of you. . . . We are well here, and think of you every day. I shall write once more, to Vienna and then, please God we shall see each other on the Rhine, and make a little music together, and talk to each other a little, and I think I shall enjoy myself a little over it. Au revoir.

Your friend,

Felix Mendelssohn Bartholdy.

As is known, Mendelssohn was a fluent and polished letter-writer. His letters to Mlle. Lind were in his fine German script as the example reproduced on pp. 53–55 shows, but he wrote excellent English as well, and many of his letters are still carefully preserved by the fortunate recipients.

Mlle. Lind was not as happy in Vienna as she was in Berlin, and wrote homesick letters to her Berlin and Swedish friends. The height to which Pokorny raised the price of seats distressed her, "nothing so high since the days of Catalani," and the poor support that was given by her colleagues made her feel that everything depended on her. And yet she could not close her eyes to the fact that her visit to the Kaiserstadt was even more successful than her best friends had expected. There was great excitement and cordiality at her Benefit Farewell, which left little doubt as to her next reception, which was to be at the end of the same year.

Before leaving Vienna Mlle. Lind sang at a *matinée* given by Taubert, the composer and conductor, contributing some of his songs and some Swedish melodies. She also assisted at a concert at the Theater am Wien in aid of a children's orphanage in which the Archduke Franz Carl was interested.

Mlle. Lind then travelled to Germany to sing for

the first time at a Rhenish Festival at Aachen (Aix-la-Chapelle) under Mendelssohn's direction. She introduced the audience to Haydn's great airs: "On mighty pens," Milton's words, which read so funnily as *Auf starkem Fittich*; and "With verdure clad," which so well displayed her powers of voice and conception. Indeed these airs and the solo and chorus, "The marvellous works," figured often in Mlle. Lind's later programmes. At Aachen she also sang in *Alexander's Feast*, but her greatest success was perhaps achieved at the Artist's Concert, in Mendelssohn's songs *Auf Flügeln des Gesanges* and *Frühlingslied*, where the combination of composer and singer was irresistible. The enthusiasm for her during the whole meeting was so great that the 1846 Festival came to be known as the "Jenny Lind Festival."

A happy band of friends had met at Aachen, among whom were counted Professor Geijer and his wife, who had come to the festival from Sweden, as a surprise to Mlle. Lind; and the whole party spent a few days on the Rhine in holiday, which no one needed more than Mendelssohn. For besides his work at the Aachen Festival, he had other engagements, and was striving to finish *Elijah*, which was on the eve of production in England. After this short rest Mlle.

Lind went to work again at Hanover, Bremen, and Hamburg, at which latter place she sang fifteen times, once for charity and once for herself.

Mlle. Lind was staying with friends in the country near Hamburg and remained there, with interruptions, for some time in the hope of recovering from the strain of so many engagements. Like Mendelssohn, she had for some time been overtaxing her strength and felt too tired to travel as far as Switzerland to join her friends the Wichmanns. Instead, she went to the adjacent seaside resort of Cuxhaven for the month of August.

In September Mlle. Lind once more entered on a heavy round of engagements in nine important German towns, beginning with Frankfort. Here, one of her first purchases was a thick and sturdy memorandum book, of immense value to her biographers, since in it she entered every engagement from the Frankfort performance of the *Sonnambula*, on September 25, 1846, to the date of her marriage in America in 1852. In this record of her activities it is interesting to count the large proportion of little "cross" marks which denote charity performances.

While at Frankfort Mlle. Lind began to receive letters from many sources in England urging her to go to London, and Mendelssohn entered the lists by

JENNY LIND.
From a Painting by Louis Asher.

asking her to receive the visit of Mr. Chorley, who was the musical critic of the *Athenæum* at the time, and was not likely to have been silent on the subject. Mr. Lumley, of Her Majesty's, was also not idle, and was enlisting Mendelssohn's powerful support for his hopes and projects, for since the close of the previous season the affairs of Her Majesty's had been in great disorder, by reason of the secession to the Covent Garden house of Lumley's chief artists. His stars, Grisi, Persiani, Rubini, Tamburini, and Mario, with Costa the conductor, had deserted him for the rival house, Lablache alone remaining faithful, and Lumley pinned his faith on a return to fortune, if only the eagerly expected Lind could be induced to appear at his house.

At this juncture Mr. Lumley travelled to Germany, called on Mendelssohn at Leipzig, and armed himself with the following letter, which he presented in person to Mlle. Lind at Darmstadt, where she was singing:

LEIPZIG, *Oct.* 12, 1846.

MY DEAR FRÄULEIN,

I intended to write to you on the day your first letter arrived; but a few hours afterwards came your second letter and Mr Lumley who brought it. All that he said to me and all that passed through my mind in connexion with it, and the different thoughts that crossed each other, made it impossible for me to write to you until to-day; and I told Mr Lumley, that if he should be coming here after his journey to Berlin, I would meanwhile think it all over carefully, and tell him whether I advise you to go to London or not.

Upon that—i.e. upon my advice—he seems to set great store and I have already told you in my former letter that the whole success of his undertaking depends upon your coming. In short, I can only repeat what I then wrote—I should like you, as far as humanly possible, to arrange, *as completely as one could wish*, *for your own comfort*, and when that has all been settled, I should like you to go there.

I should have strongly urged Mr Lumley to speak clearly and exactly about money matters; because that is a very serious point in England; and because you could and should make such terms as no one else could at the moment, since you are the *only* one upon whom the whole thing depends. But—do not be angry with me! I had not the courage to do this, not even for you, though I know that you understand that kind of thing even less than I do—in other words, not at all. But it is such a very sore point with me, and I rejoice so much when I have nothing to hear or say about it, that I could not bring the words to my lips. And at last I thought "It is not my province," and so, after all I let it pass.

Therefore I can only repeat, it must all be as is just and right for you.

Nevertheless, you will certainly meet with such a reception there, that you will be able to think of it with pleasure throughout your future life. When the English once entertain a personal liking for anyone, I believe no people are more friendly, more cordial, or more constant. For, as I have told you before, I have noticed that they entertain this true feeling thereon, not only about your singing, but about your personality, and your whole being, and upon this last they even set more store than upon the singing itself. And this is as it should be. In my opinion, therefore, it cannot be doubted that you will be received there as you deserve—more warmly, enthusiastically, and heartily than, perhaps in all your former experience; and you have experienced a good deal in that way. You will, therefore, give your friends great pleasure if you go there; and I for my part would be very glad indeed if you were to go. . . .

I am selfish too in my advice, for I hope that we shall there meet in this world again. While still in England I had half promised to return in April; had I only known that you would be there at the time or be likely to go, how much more willingly I should have settled it. Mr Lumley, also, has, in the kindest manner proposed that I should compose an opera for him next May, and I could only answer that on the same day on which I succeeded in getting a good libretto, on a good subject, I would begin to write the music; and that in doing so I would be fulfilling my greatest wish. He hopes soon to be able to procure such a libretto, and has already taken some decided steps in the matter. God grant that some good results may follow.

From Mme. Birch-Pfeiffer I have not heard a single word for some time. In the meantime the music-paper and finely nibbed pens are lying on the table — and wait.

But, apart from this, I hope, as I have told you, to visit

London again next spring, and what a pleasure it will be to me to witness there the most brilliant and hearty reception that can possibly fall to an artist's lot! For I know full well that that is what your reception will be, and it will be great fun for me, that you yourself will be the fêted artist.

For myself, I am doing well; but during the three weeks since I returned here, I have done scarcely anything but rest, so tired was I—and still am sometimes—with the work that preceded the journey to England, and the journey itself. The performance of my *Elijah* was the best first performance that I have ever heard of any one of my compositions. There was so much go, and swing in the way the people played and sang and listened. I wish you had been there. But I have now fallen back in to the concert trouble, and can neither get true rest nor quietness here. So I have built myself a grand castle in the air; namely, to travel, next summer, with my whole family, in my favourite country—which as you know is Switzerland—and then to study uninterruptedly for two months on one of the lakes, living in the open air. If God gives us health, we will carry out this plan; and when I think of such a quiet time in the country after all the hurry and bustle, and all the brightness of a London season, and remember how dear both of them are to me, and how well they please me, I almost wish that the spring were already here, and that I was taking my seat in a railway carriage.

And now, to-day I have a request to make. Write to me *at once* when you have come to a decision concerning England, and tell me everything with all the details, for you know how much it interests me. Before all things, then, write to me from time to time, and think kindly of me sometimes.

As for myself, you know that I am and remain,

Your friend,

FELIX MENDELSSOHN BARTHOLDY.

This, no doubt, is a very charming letter, but we should not call it very helpful in advising her as to *what* she was to arrange so "completely for her own comfort as to be just and right for herself."

The performance of the *Elijah* to which Mendelssohn refers in this letter was its first performance, and took place at Birmingham on August 26, 1846. This was Mendelssohn's ninth visit to England.

To Mr. Lumley's great relief this letter of Mendelssohn's, added to the pressure of her English and other friends, seems at last to have broken down Mlle. Lind's resistance, if not her fears. Mr. Lumley was offering her generous terms as well as shouldering eventual trouble with Mr. Bunn over the unfulfilled contract which had so haunted Mlle. Lind. Lumley offered a high price for those days—£4,800 for the season, a furnished house, horses and a carriage. He also offered to pay for a visit to Italy, should she desire to rest and study there, before the London season, of which offer she did not avail herself, preferring to get the ordeal of her debut in London over, as soon as her Continental engagements would permit.

With her signature to the contract, which this time was a real one, signed by both parties, the question of her appearing at Her Majesty's Theatre was decided at last, and when Mlle. Lind left Darmstadt she had committed herself to the most important engagement, and prepared the way for the most solid artistic triumph associated with her name.

She arrived at Munich to give seven operatic performances between October 23 and November 9, and stayed in the house of Professor Kaulbach, the well-known Bavarian painter, where she was treated by him and his wife as a beloved daughter and made no less at home than she was with the Wichmanns in Berlin. Her safe position in a Bavarian family also saved her from an invitation to sing at Court, where at that time the notorious Lola Montez was a prominent personage.

In a letter to Mme. Wichmann, she thanks her for having sent her some rouge (which the critics were recommending her to use more freely). She says that she has taken Mendelssohn's advice to go to London, and hopes to go to Italy for a few weeks first. She ends her letter:

Besides this all goes well with me here, as everywhere. I am beginning to feel accustomed to this, though I cannot conceive what it is that satisfies the people. But that is God's doing! Thine for ever,

JENNY.

During Mlle. Lind's first visit to Vienna, Mendelssohn had introduced his friend Franz Hauser, a well-known bass singer, who was a teacher of singing in Vienna. He was a great help and encouragement to her at the time of her Vienna debut, and in return for the introduction, kept Mendelssohn *au courant* with all that went on.

Now Mlle. Lind found him at Munich, where he had become Director of the Conservatoire. He and Mendelssohn were both advising Mlle. Lind not to go to Italy, as she wished. She had studied Italian on her first visit to Vienna, and they considered that her pronunciation required no more tuition than Lablache could give her in London and they thought that she ought to spare herself the fatigue of travelling first to Italy and then to London. So the Italian journey faded away and she gave herself up to the present, and her engagements in Munich and other South German towns.

On December 18 Mlle. Lind sang the part of Susanna in *Le Nozze di Figaro* for the first time out of Sweden. She subsequently sang it four times in London.

Her farewell to Munich was in a performance of the *Creation*, the second benefit for the orchestra, and she gave it on Christmas Day as her way of celebrating the festival and helping others.

Mlle. Lind opened her second season in Vienna on January 7, 1847, with a first performance there of *La Figlia del Reggimento*, and the newspapers were less cautious than previously in their share of the now universal European admiration for her.

The Schumanns were then staying in Vienna and giving concerts of deep artistic interest. Three were already over when Mlle. Lind arrived, but she offered to sing at the fourth, and the demand for seats was greatly increased. From Mme. Schumann's diary we may quote some extracts of the 11th and 12th of January:

Gave my 4th and last concert, which was full to suffocation, so that many people could not get places. Jenny Lind sang wonderfully. One can never forget such achievements.

[Next day.] Called on Jenny Lind, who immediately on our entrance called out: "Will you not give another concert and let me sing?" We stayed a long time, and I sat as if rooted to my place. I am so fond of her; she is, for me the warmest, noblest being that I have found among artists, and

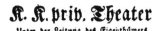

K. K. priv. Theater an der Wien.

Unter der Leitung des Eigenthümers Franz Pokorny.

Im Laufe dieser Woche findet die

Erste Gastvorstellung der Demoiselle

Jenny Lind,

in

Marie, die Tochter des Regiments,

Oper in drei Aufzügen, Musik von Donizetti, Statt.

Das Nähere wird der Anschlagezettel am Tage der Vorstellung enthalten.

Preise:

Eine Loge . . .	20 fl.	— kr.	Ein Sperrsitz in der 3. Gallerie	1 fl.	20 kr.
Ein Parquet-Sitz . .	5 »	— »	Eintritt in das Parterre oder in die 1. Gallerie . .	1 »	20 »
Ein Sperrsitz im Parterre oder in der ersten Gallerie	2 »	30 »	Eintritt in die 2. Gallerie	1 »	— »
Ein Sperrsitz in der 2. Gallerie	2 »	— »	» » » 3. Gallerie	— »	40 »
			» » » 4. Gallerie	— »	20 »

Um den vielseitig geäußerten Wünschen zu begegnen, sind die Parquet-Sitze, so wie bei den früheren Gastvorstellungen der Dlle. Jenny Lind, hergestellt worden.

Vormerkungen auf Logen, Parquet- und Sperrsitze werden nur allein in dem gewöhnlichen Logen- und Sperrsitz-Verkaufslokale in der Stadt, angenommen.

Zur ersten Gastvorstellung der Dlle. Jenny Lind, sind sämmtliche Logen, Parquet- und Sperrsitze bereits vergeben.

Jede, die obigen festgesetzten Preise übersteigende Forderung, so wie jede in Beziehung auf die vorgemerkten Logen, Parquet- und Sperrsitze etwa vorkommende Beeinträchtigung, bittet der Gefertigte, ihm gütigst und unverweilt anzeigen zu wollen.

Franz Pokorny, Theater-Unternehmer.

Announcement of the Vienna Performance, Jan. 7, 1847.

how can I ever forget her—one must know her thoroughly to love her as I do.

As well as singing for the Schumanns, Mlle. Lind sang at a concert for little Wilhelmina Neruda (afterwards Lady Hallé), who though then little more than six years old, had already made a great reputation in Vienna as a child-violinist. And she sang at many Court and charity concerts during the season.

Meyerbeer was also in Vienna with a revised version of *Das Feldlager*, which he renamed *Vielka*, after the heroine. Its success was triumphant, and it ran for thirteen nights, and the famous trio for Vielka and two flutes, afterwards transferred to *L'Etoile du Nord*, has become a show piece. Incredible as it may seem after all her successes, Mlle. Lind was so dissatisfied with her own performance, that when her friends the von Jaegers hurried to her dressing-room to congratulate her on her new triumph, they found her bathed in tears of penitence at what she considered her imperfect singing. Not even Meyerbeer's thanks and assurances could convince her otherwise.

On this same evening a great compliment was paid her by the presentation of a lovely medal in gold, silver, and bronze "From the Art Lovers of Vienna," and we must hope that this gift effectually dried her tears.

Moreover, a further proof of appreciation was conferred on her by the Emperor Ferdinand's appointment of her as Court singer. The words of the document were couched in graceful terms, recognizing not only her talents as an artist but her philanthropy in assisting benevolent causes.

As we have quoted Mme. Schumann's words about Mlle. Lind, we would like to show that the affection was mutual. To Mme. Wichmann in Berlin Mlle. Lind wrote:

VIENNA, *Jan.* 20, 1847.

I know so well your love and self-denying kindness for me, that I do not for a moment fear that you will be vexed if I send someone to your house. You will not be angry, will you? I mean the Schumanns.

You know of course that her talent is altogether splendid; for you have often heard of her as Clara Wieck. They are two such excellent and noble, really noble persons, that they will give you great pleasure. Please, Dearly-Beloved, receive these two dear people kindly, and as friends, for your own sake and for mine. The wife is very sensitive, and you will see that she is quite an exceptional woman. He is a composer *plein d'esprit* and modest to the last degree. I asked them if they had any acquaintances in Berlin; and they seemed to me to have no real ones. And then it was that I thought of you; and you may well know how grateful I shall be.

Ah, yes! When shall I see you again? Mon Dieu!

This longing for rest grows upon me, almost beyond measure; but time passes quickly, and no mortal will be as glad as I, when I am but free.

The next letter is written three weeks later, also to Mme. Wichmann:

VIENNA, *Feb.* 13, 1847.

What can you be thinking about! I, going to Paris! Who could have told you that? I am not only not going to Paris, but it seems as if I shall not even go to London. Bunn will not give up the contract; and I cannot go there unless he does, for he actually threatens to put me in prison!!! I tell you, Amalie, I should be wild with joy if I had not to go there! Suppose it fell out so. They have made me all possible offers from Paris; but I did not for a moment think it over. The stage I will leave—and I shall then want nothing else in the world. . . . I rejoice that it gives me so much pleasure to hear of Viardot Garcia's success in Berlin. I have never been envious for a moment. Tell Taubert so; he thinks I am rather weak on that point.

It seems extraordinary that anyone could have put the absurd notion of imprisonment into Mlle. Lind's head, but there is strong evidence that she really did believe it, and was terrified. She had empowered her London friends to purchase her safety from the redoubtable Bunn with an offer of no less than £2,000, which offer Mr. Bunn refused to accept.

While on one side of the Channel Mlle. Lind was

tormented with fears for her own personal safety, Mr. Lumley was racked with anxiety concerning the fate of Her Majesty's, and the bid he had made for salvation, dependent on the appearance of a timid prima donna.

At this critical juncture Mr. Edward Lewin, Mrs. Grote's brother, who was equally trusted by Mr. Lumley and Miss Lind, volunteered a journey to Vienna in the hope of reassuring the lady. The accounts he sent home were, however, so far from favourable that Mr. Lumley felt it his duty to undertake the journey himself, and though he could ill be spared at home, on the last night before the Easter recess he slipped away, in evening dress between the acts, to catch the Calais train. He travelled straight through till he found himself in Vienna, face to face with the object of his search, and never left her again till on their journey to London he had got her as far as Calais, where he left her to rest in the charge of Mr. Lewin, the battle won.

CHAPTER VII

1847

WHILE the subscribers were anxiously awaiting Mlle. Lind's appearance at the Opera another musical event was taking place, for Mendelssohn was paying his tenth and last visit to London at the invitation of the Sacred Harmonic Society to conduct four performances of the *Elijah* at Exeter Hall. He was staying with his friend Mr. Klingemann at 4 Hobart Place, Eaton Square, and was easily persuaded to prolong his stay so as to welcome Mlle. Lind on her arrival. On the day that she really was due, Mendelssohn and Mrs. Grote anxiously patrolled Eccleston Street, outside Mrs. Grote's house, where Mlle. Lind was to stay, watching the corner of the street. Great was their relief when at last two heavily laden cabs came round it, and deposited safely a rather tired and frightened Mlle. Lind.

That same evening at the Opera all eyes were levelled at Box 48 on the grand tier when it became known that Mlle. Lind actually was in the house in

Mrs. Grote's box. Mr. Lumley visited the box to introduce his faithful Signor Lablache, who had all along urged him to capture the shy "nightingale," and a few days later the same party dined together at Mrs. Grote's, with the addition of Mendelssohn, who made music with Mlle. Lind, once more, after dinner. As alas! the sands of Mendelssohn's life were running out, we would like to give almost the last of his tributes to Mlle. Lind, when he played Beethoven's G major Concerto, on April 26 at the Philharmonic, with Queen Victoria present. When complimented by a friend on his specially fine rendering of the Concerto, he replied, with a smile, that he was anxious to please two ladies in the audience, the Queen and Mlle. Lind.

As Barnum did, later, in America, so Lumley now thought fit to whet the curiosity of the public as to the new star he was introducing to it, and Mlle. Lind arrived in London in a blaze of advertisement, entirely distasteful to her nature. She once more suffered great anxiety at facing a new audience in strange surroundings, and only the consciousness of Lumley's need carried her through to a decision to appear on May 4, making her debut in *Roberto il Diavolo.*

The excitement of the Jenny Lind fever of those days is now a matter of history. From an early hour of the afternoon the colonnade adjoining the old theatre, as it still does the new—Her Majesty's was crowded by fashionable people in evening dress waiting for pit places, all others having long been disposed of. When the curtain went up, Royalty sat in their box, and many celebrities, including Mendelssohn, sat in the stalls, and Mlle. Lind's appearance in her pilgrim's dress was greeted with a burst of applause, not usually given in anticipation, but rather in recognition, of success. Such a reception both affected and surprised her, but she soon recovered her self-possession, the part giving her time to do so, while others carried on the action. The most experienced critics were taken aback by the prima donna's fresh conception of the part of Alice and her complete forgetfulness of self, quite apart from the magic of her voice and singing, and the artist, on her side, from the first appreciated rightly her new public and in that appreciation forgot her fears.

The whole performance called forth one long-sustained ovation, led by the Queen, who expressed her admiration to Mr. Lumley. There could be no doubts for the future of his enterprise whatever attractions the rival company might put forth. The management was saved, for Mlle. Lind's triumph was as lasting as it was complete.

The Times of May 5 criticized the performance with full appreciation, of which we give the following extracts:

If our expectations were great, we must say that they were fully realized. The delicious quality of the organ—the rich gushing tone—was something entirely new and fresh. . . . The sustained notes, swelling with full richness, and fading down to the softest piano without losing one iota of their quality, being delicious when loud, delicious when whispered, dwelt in the public ear, and reposed in the public heart. The shake, *mezza voce*, with which she concluded the pretty air " Quand je quittais la Normandie " was perfectly wonderful from its rapidity and equality. . . .

And the impression she made as an actress was no less profound. There is no conventionality about her, no seizing the strong points of a character and letting the rest drop. . . . Her whole conception is a fine histrionic study, of which every feature is equally good.

It is nice to have Mlle. Lind's own account of events, so we will give a letter which she wrote to Judge Munthe five days later:

LONDON, *May* 10*th*, 1847.

It is always a pleasure to write to my good guardian and fatherlike friend; but this time I write with a lighter heart than usual, because I have succeeded so well in this my last undertaking, which was to make my way here in London, in spite of all the difficulties and intrigues that people have tried to throw in my way. I appeared as Alice in *Roberto* in the 4th of this month, and I cannot describe the sympathy and enthusiasm with which I was received—and, to my astonishment, well understood! I am so happy, and find things so pleasant, that there is perhaps no being under the sun so happy as I.

And to other friends she wrote of herself as "happy and satisfied" with Lumley as "a good friend" and Lablache as "a kind father," and the general public as "spoiling her." With the mention of that fine singer, with his magnificent voice and splendid art and bearing, we would like to note the fact that in all the operas in which Lablache sang with Mlle. Lind he was the one of her fellow-artists who always received due appreciation and appeared with her before the curtain.

Mlle. Lind lived in a little house called Clairville Cottage, among what were then Brompton market gardens, quite near the house in which she lived during the last ten years of her life, and from the first she was accepted by all that was best in the social life of London, from Queen Victoria downwards. The Duke of Wellington was one of her ardent admirers, and seldom missed an Opera night when she sang. He occupied a box next the stage, and always arrived in time to see the curtain go up. To anyone less engrossed in her art it might have been disconcerting

CLAIRVILLE COTTAGE, BROMPTON.

Jenny Lind's first home in London.

to be addressed by name, with an inquiry for her health, whenever she made her first entry for the evening. The Duke used to take Mlle. Lind out riding, with a groom in attendance, as was the custom in those days, to Richmond Park or among the rhododendrons in Wimbledon Park.

Mlle. Lind sang in *Roberto il Diavolo* three times, before appearing, on May 13, for the first time in the *Sonnambula* which, as sung by her, became the favourite opera of the season. It was given again and again to crowded houses with triumphant success.

By this time I think we have quite realized that Mlle. Lind's greatness in opera lay in the power and sincerity of her playing combined with the perfection of her voice and method. In the *Sonnambula* it is worth noting the fact that whereas it was usual for prima donnas to send a "super" across the plank in the sleep-walking scene, Mlle. Lind always went herself, carrying her candle with her eyes fixed in sleep, the whole a perilous and nerve-racking undertaking added to the singer's vocal efforts.

After four performances of *Roberto* and four of the *Sonnambula* the management ventured to present an opera entirely unknown to the London public. This was Donizetti's *Figlia del Reggimento*, originally written in 1840 for the Paris Opera Comique, and subsequently brought out in the form of an Italian opera. It does not show the composer at his best, though it has grace and vivacity. The character of Maria is in striking contrast to the other rôles that had made Mlle. Lind famous, and it is a tribute to her art that with such slender means for its foundation she should have held her audience spellbound the moment she appeared. And so it came about that of all the operas presented during this eventful season the *Figlia del Reggimento* became one of the chief favourites.

June 15 was a memorable night in the annals of Her Majesty's Theatre for the Queen and Prince Consort honoured the old house with a State visit, and Mlle. Lind appeared by Royal Command, for the first time in London, in the rôle of Norma. The performance was a brilliant and successful one, but the London newspapers were divided in opinion on the merits of Mlle. Lind's conception and its difference from that with which Mme. Grisi had long made them familiar. The fairest critiques allowed merit and high praise to both artists, but it is curious to note that though on the Continent Norma was one of Mlle. Lind's most successful rôles, here it was less popular than either Amina or Alice, in the *Sonnambula* and *Roberto* respectively.

PROGRAMME OF

HER MAJESTY'S THEATRE.

By Authority.

TUESDAY EVENING, JULY 13, 1847,

Will be performed BELLINI's celebrated Opera, entitled

LA SONNAMBULA.

AMINA . . . . . . Mlle. JENNY LIND.
LISA . . . . Madame SOLARI.
COUNT RODOLPHO . . . . Signor F. LABLACHE.
ALESSIO . . . . Signor GIUBILEI.
ELVINO . . . . Signor GARDONI.

To conclude with the highly successful New Ballet Divertissement, by M. PERROT, the Music by Signor BAJETTI, of the Imperial Theatre, La Scala, Milan, and M. NADAUD, entitled

LES ELEMENS.

The Scenery by Mr. CHARLES MARSHALL.

THE FIRE . . . . . . Mlle. CARLOTTA GRISI
(Her Last Appearance but One).
THE WATER . . Mlle. CAROLINA ROSATI.
THE AIR . . . . Mlle. CERITO.
THE EARTH . . Mlles. CASSAN, JAMES, THEVENOT, and HONORE.

The New Opera,

I MASNIDIERI,

Composed expressly for her Majesty's Theatre by Signor VERDI, is in active rehearsal, and will be produced forthwith.

Principal Characters by Mlle. JENNY LIND, and Signori GARDONI, COLETTI, BOUCHE, and LABLACHE.

Madame TAGLIONI has arrived, and will shortly appear.

THE FREE LIST IS SUSPENDED, THE PUBLIC PRESS EXCEPTED.

Pit Tickets may be obtained as usual at the Box-office of the Theatre, price 10s. 6d. each.

Applications for Boxes, Pit Stalls, and Tickets to be made at the Box-office, at the Theatre.

Doors open at Half-past Seven o'Clock, the Opera to commence at Eight.

It is interesting to know, on good authority, that two years later Mme. Grisi herself made the remarkable and generous statement that after she had heard Mlle. Lind sing Norma she realized that there could be two conceptions of the part, equally genuine.

During Mlle. Lind's first Vienna season we read of the correspondence passing on the subject of an opera which Mr. Lumley had commissioned Mendelssohn to write and which was virtually promised to Her Majesty's opera subscribers.

But Mendelssohn's search for a libretto seems to have been no more successful now than it had been ten years before. There is a letter from him to Mr. W. Chappell, of 50 New Bond Street, even then, in which he accepts an offer to write an opera for him; but his conditions as to the nature of the libretto were as follows:

> I do not wish it to be a subject with fairies or other romantic modern spirits; I wish it to be very substantially human; historical or else fictitious—but at all events lively and dramatic in every little part. In fact I wish for a libretto which gets me in to music at once, not one which I must set first.

This letter is dated Leipzig, December 26, 1837, and in the season of 1847 Mr. Lumley was faced with the necessity of satisfying his clients some other way for their disappointment as to a Mendelssohn opera. In his perplexity he hit on a new opera just completed by Verdi, founded on Schiller's "Robbers," and called in Italian *I Masnadieri*.

With Mlle. Lind in the chief part, the opera was given on July 22, 1847, and failed to please, though Mlle. Lind scored her usual personal success. In the subject of the libretto it was not possible to focus interest on the heroine, as in the *Figlia del Reggimento*. In the Donizetti opera people crowded the house, not so much to hear his music as to hear Jenny Lind sing; in *I Masnadieri* they could not concentrate on the singer.

Mlle. Lind's next appearance, as Susanna in *Le Nozze de Figaro*, was a welcome change from the gloom of Schiller's "Robbers." She had studied the part deeply, and sang it as she felt Mozart would have wished it sung, never deviating in the smallest detail either in singing or acting from the indications of the score. So great was Mlle. Lind's love for Mozart's music that she always spoke of him as "the Divine Mozart" in the same way that in later years when she studied Bach she alluded to him as "that blessèd old man."

From the Meyerbeer and lesser lights of her youth, to the Bach she loved in her later years, was the wide range of Mlle. Lind's knowledge and tastes. Of

Handel and Haydn she became a famous interpreter after she had left the stage, and devoted herself to oratorio singing, and her manner of singing the songs of Schubert, Schumann, and Mendelssohn has been mentioned elsewhere in our story. Brahms was after her day, though she had met him before he became famous. Wagner she entirely failed to appreciate, as she never could dissociate a man from his works, and considered his writing as detrimental to the voice.

Mlle. Lind's sympathies were entirely with the Italian school of singing as against the German, but she never subscribed to the idea that English was a language that could not be sung. As evidence we have her predilection for singing oratorio after she had left the stage, and her splendid declamation of the text before even her spoken English was faultless.

In her contract with Mr. Lumley there was a clause which precluded Mlle. Lind from taking part in any public concert during the London season; a wise clause, since it would have been highly imprudent for an artist on whom so much depended, to have added to the fatigue and excitement of her appearances at the Opera. But an exception had been made, through Mendelssohn's foresight, to permit of her obeying Royal Commands. Thus, during the Season, she was able to sing twice at Buckingham Palace and once at Osborne, besides taking part in a concert given by Queen Adelaide at Marlborough House.

We have been permitted to see Queen Victoria's notes on these concerts, which gave both the items Mlle. Lind sang, and the remarkable impression she made on a concert platform as distinguished from the Opera stage. Special mention is made of the unrivalled charm of the Swedish songs, sung to her own accompaniment, the effect of the softness and finish being extraordinary and almost stunning. Her Majesty on each occasion conversed at length with Mlle. Lind, who spoke from the first of her intention to leave the stage. On the Queen's expressing regret for the loss to art, Mlle. Lind replied that whether she left the stage or not she hoped to return to England and continue to deserve the kindness she received.

We do not feel that we are unduly anticipating events when we say here, that however brilliant Mlle. Lind's stage career was, in London as well as in Berlin and Vienna, it did not represent the whole of her art life. When the London season ended her successes in this country were only beginning. Her fame had penetrated to the farthest corners of the kingdom, and the inhabitants of the great towns were impatient to judge for themselves whether the rumours that reached them were exaggerated or not.

So, a provincial tour was organized during August and September (1847) on her own account, but admirably managed by Mr. Edward Lewin, Mrs. George Grote's brother, who was so valuable a friend to Mlle. Lind at this time. She knew very little English as yet, and could certainly not have contended with the business side of the tour, and Mr. Lewin was perfectly at home with the Swedish language, having lived in Sweden. They had secured the assistance of Signor Gardoni and Signor Lablache and his wife, as well as an efficient orchestra, conducted by Mr. Balfe, and with these popular and excellent artists Mlle. Lind extended her tour to Scotland, and was fêted and made much of, everywhere. But in one particular town, her reception was so cordial, and the friendships she made, so true and lasting, that we must give a fuller account than our space allows in general.

Mlle. Lind had received during her London season what must have been surely a unique invitation for an opera singer, written by the Bishop of Norwich himself, to stay with him and Mrs. Stanley at the Palace during her projected visit to Norwich. One sentence ran that "it would be a great gratification to make acquaintance with one whose high character and principles, from all he had heard, were on a par with her superior talents." The invitation was accepted and the warmth of her reception was remembered with pleasure all her life.

Besides the original scheme of two concerts Mlle. Lind gave an extra morning one, for the benefit of those who had been unable to pay the high prices ot the other concerts.

Bishop Stanley's son, afterwards Dean of Westminster, provides us with almost the greatest testimony to Mlle. Lind's personality, apart from her gifts of music. He cared little for, and knew less of, music, and yet his judgment of her character, as looking on her talents as gifts and not merits, and her desire, not only to keep herself unspotted, but to elevate the tone of her profession, was eminently true, and he describes her as having "the manners of a princess and the simplicity of a child."

Bishop Stanley of Norwich is often quoted as having, from religious motives, influenced Mlle. Lind to leave the stage, but this is not really true, since her determination to do so was formed long before she met him, as evidenced in letters and speech to her friends.

While on the subject of Norwich we may anticipate

events by recording another visit in the following January, when Mlle. Lind gave two charity concerts, the original nucleus of the Children's Hospital which to this day, though entirely remodelled, bears her name. (She sang in Norwich again in 1862.)

After the visit to Norwich, as described above, Mlle. Lind sang at Clifton, Bristol, and Exeter, before returning to London to embark for Hamburg *en route* for a brief engagement in Berlin; but the seed of her love for England had been sown, to bear fruit, as we shall see later.

She left behind in England a splendid reputation, and extensive personal interest, and she also carried with her as the result of five months' work a larger sum of money than she had previously been mistress of.

As will be seen from the accompanying broadsheet, during the "Jenny Lind fever," the most incongruous things were named after Mlle. Lind: cigars (which she abhorred), servants' caps, melons, and flies for trout-fishing, etc. During the first Alaska gold-rush a baker (probably a Swede) announced on the door of his shanty that he made "Jenny Lind" cakes, and to-day there is still, at Hastings, a prosperous public-house bearing her name.

THE JENNY LIND MANIA.

E. Hodges, from PITTS, Wholesale Toy & Marbe Warehouse, 31, Dudley Street, Seven Dials.

OH! is there not a pretty fuss,
In London all around,
About the Sweedish Nightengale,
The talk of all the town,
Each Square and Street as through you pass,
Aloud with praises ring
About this pretty singing bird,
The famous Jenny Lind,

CHORUS.

For she turns each heart, and turns each head,
Of those who hear her sing
And she is turning all her notes to gold,
Is famous Jenny Lind.

All singers she out-shines,
None can with her come nigh.
And some declares that she must be,
An angel from the sky,
She sings so sweet, aud sings so loud,
As I've heard people say,
You might hear her from the Haymarket.
As far as Boteny Bay.

As to a liquor shop you go,
To drink your wine or gin,
The Landlord begs that you will taste
His famons Jenny Lind,
And I heard a dustman t'other day.
As he his bell did ring,
Instead of bawling out "Dust O!"
Called out for Jenny Lind.

P—A—and our loving Queen,
Had such a precious row
Because he at the Op ra House,
To Jenny Lind did bow,
Sye beat him round and roual the house,
All with the rolling pin
Till he said, my dear, I will not look,
Or wink at Jenny Lind,

Now every thing is Jenny Lind,
That comes out new each day.
There's Jenny Lind shawls and bonnets too,
For those who cash can pay,
Jenny Lind's coats and Waistcoats
Shirts, whiskers too, and stocks,
Jenny Lind's gowns and petticoats,
And bustles such a lot.

If to a butcher's shop you go,
To buy a joint of meat,
It's buy oh, buy my Jenuy Lind,
She's tender and she's sweet,
And the greasy little butcher's boys,
Sing with a knowing grin.
Eightpence a pound this splendid leg,
It is fit for Jenny Lind,

The gents smoke nought but Jenny Lind.
For so they name Cigars,
And shopboys for to come out slap,
Smoke Jenny Lind by halves,
And ladies who a shoping go,
To the Mercer's will drop in,
And ask for a yard and a half of silk
Cut off of Jenny Lind.

Now to conclude and end my song,
For I think it is almost time,
Success to the little singing bird,
The subject of my rhymes;
I have seen some wonders in my time,
And singing birds some scores,
But I never new a singing bird,
Wear petticoats before,

CHAPTER VIII

1847–1848

RELLSTAB gave an account of Mlle. Lind's farewell to the Berlin stage on the occasion of her benefit on October 17, 1847. He deplores her decision to leave the stage at the height of her powers, while appreciating her motives and intention to devote herself to concerts and oratorio in future, but neither he nor anyone else was capable of making her change her mind on this subject.

Her last notes at the Berlin Opera House were heard on October 18, when she gave a concert for the benefit of the members of the chorus. It was for this occasion that Taubert composed the song *Ich muss nun einmal singen.* It was intended as a show-piece, and the German words fitted the music which was written for them, but as frequently sung in America, in an English translation, the words leave much to be desired. Following the example of the Emperor of Austria, King Frederick William of Prussia, after a Court concert at Sans Souci, appointed

Mlle. Lind his Court singer, and wrote with his own hand to inform her of this fact in much simpler language and less correct French than such documents usually present. From Berlin Mlle. Lind went to Hamburg to sing the *Figlia* once only, and then left for Stockholm with her mind full of philanthropic aims.

With the vivid recollection of her own young life, one of the chief aims now before Mlle. Lind was to provide for others, against some of the difficulties which she had encountered for lack of means, at crucial times. For we remember how she overstrained her voice and powers in working to collect the means for her journey to Paris to study with Garcia. From the moment that she won her place in European fame, Mlle. Lind never sang again in Sweden for her own benefit, and perhaps on this occasion she felt a special need for efforts to do good. It may be that the religious influences under which she had come in England had deepened her already simple piety, but she became alarmed during this winter of her return to Sweden at the lack of seriousness that she met on all sides. Her three years of travel had given her an insight into moral perils which she herself shunned, and she hoped to help young aspirants to the stage to escape unwholesome influences, by founding a college which would be their home and shelter.

The news of her determination to leave the stage had given rise to rumours that she had once more over-fatigued her voice, but it was in its normal splendour, and she sang during the winter in thirty-five operatic performances, and in fourteen concerts in aid of various old friends and associates, as well as for public charities. At her last two appearances as Norma the tickets were sold by public auction. For the last time, on April 12 (1848), in the part of Norma, Mlle. Lind waited in the wings of her old dramatic home for the step forward that should carry her in to the roar of welcome, and we are told that she surpassed herself. When she came before the curtain at the close the whole audience rose and many an eye was wet.

Notwithstanding the raised prices and crowded performances, the resulting sums were insufficient for the realization of her plans, and she had to modify them. The capital she had acquired, together with accruing interest, were therefore left in the care of trustees for some years, and it was not until the year 1863 that they felt justified in instituting the Travelling Scholarships that to-day bear Jenny Lind's name. Up to 1925 there have been thirty holders of the scholarship,

From a Daguerrotype by Kilburn.

not only musicians but also scholars from the Academy of Fine Arts. Mlle. Lind, after her American tour, also founded a Geijer Scholarship at Upsala and another, bearing Bishop Tegner's name, at Lund University.

It is well known that besides many private charities Mlle. Lind's public benefactions were very numerous. Many evidences of gratitude in England took the form of handsome gifts and testimonials from the institutions benefited, though she always deprecated such gifts and never accepted any from private sources.

The final season on the home boards had ended, and Mlle. Lind was due to leave for London for a long period. In many letters of that date she expressed her pleasure in the thought of her next London season, and looked forward to a happy summer in her little Clairville Cottage, all the more as her old master, Herr Berg, his wife and daughter, were going too.

CHAPTER IX

1848–1849

HER Majesty's Theatre opened for the season of 1848 on February 19 with Verdi's *Ernani*, with Mlle. Cruvelli making her debut before an English audience.

It was confidently expected that Mlle. Lind would make her reappearance directly after the Easter recess, on April 29, but at her earnest request her *rentrée* was postponed, as explained in Mr. Lumley's following amusing letter:

Yes, Jenny Lind was amongst us, and the most eager expectations were raised as to her first appearance. When, how, what would she play? were the questions impatiently asked. It was earnestly desired that she should appear on Saturday the 29th of April. But, with the natural tendency of the Scandinavian temperament to believe in occult influences, she laid great stress on the fact that the 4th May—the ensuing Thursday—was the date of her first appearance on the London boards; and she therefore decided that, on the 4th of May—and not before the 4th May—she would celebrate her return to the boards of Her Majesty's Theatre.

The opera chosen for Mlle. Lind's *rentrée* was the *Sonnambula* on May 4 (1848), and we have Chopin's impression of her in the letter he wrote to his friend Grzymala:

I have been to the Italian Opera where Jenny Lind appeared in *La Sonnambula*, and the Queen showed herself for the first time to the people after a long retirement. Both were, of course, of great interest to me; more especially, however, the Duke of Wellington, who, like an old, faithful dog in a cottage, sat in a box below his crowned mistress. I have also made Jenny Lind's personal acquaintance. When a few days afterwards I paid her a visit, she received me in the most amiable manner, and sent me an excellent "stall" for the Opera, where I was capitally seated and heard excellently.

This Swede is an original from head to foot. She does not show herself in the ordinary light, but in the magic rays of the aurora borealis. Her singing is infallibly pure and true, but, above all I admire her "piano" passages, the charm of which is indescribable.

The admiration of the two artists was mutual, and Mlle. Lind's did not end with Chopin's death, but increased as years passed, and she became better acquainted with his works through her husband. For Mr. Otto Goldschmidt had studied with Chopin, and was present at the last concert given by him, in the Salle Pleyel in Paris shortly before his death. After her marriage Mme. Goldschmidt was very fond of singing an arrangement of Chopin's Mazurkas which her husband had made for the voice.

We cannot again give accounts of the operas in which Mlle. Lind repeated her triumphs of the previous year. Interest continued unabated. Fresh food for admiration was, moreover, found in her first appearance in *Lucia di Lammermoor*, in which her histrionic powers had full play in the madness of the last scene, and the opera was given twelve times during the season.

Mlle. Lind also appeared in Donizetti's opera bouffe *L'Elisir d'Amore*, ably supported by Lablache in one of his genial parts, producing most piquant effects in the scenes in which he was associated with the prima donna.

But Mlle. Lind's final and last new rôle was of a very different character, as Elvira in *I Puritani*. Her rendering of the air *Qui la voce* was one of her life-long *chefs d'œuvre*, never to be forgotten by those who heard it, and the cadence she composed for it was one of the finest and most original passages of *fioratura* with which she used to ornament the Italian airs which she liked best.

The success of *I Puritani* was enormous, and it was

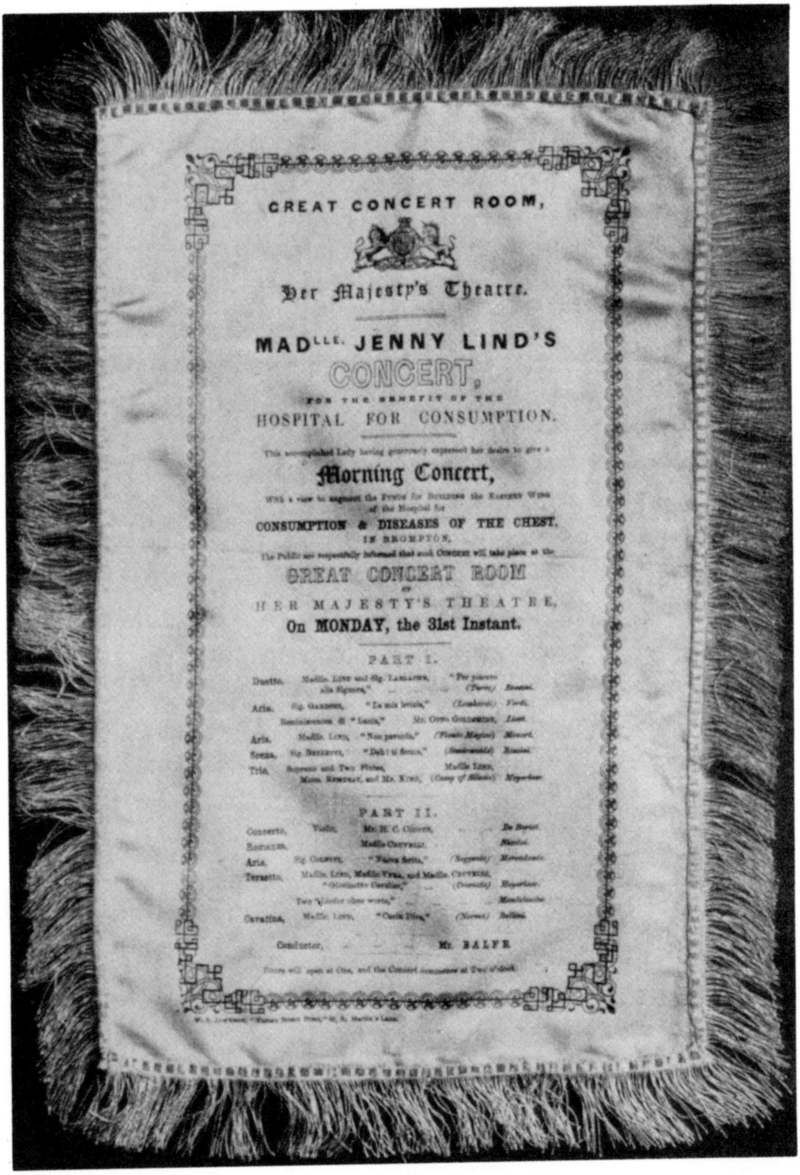

GREAT CONCERT ROOM,

Her Majesty's Theatre.

MADLLE. JENNY LIND'S

CONCERT,

FOR THE BENEFIT OF THE

HOSPITAL FOR CONSUMPTION.

Morning Concert,

CONSUMPTION & DISEASES OF THE CHEST,

IN BROMPTON.

GREAT CONCERT ROOM

OF

HER MAJESTY'S THEATRE,

On MONDAY, the 31st Instant.

PART I.

Duetto.

Aria.

Aria.

Scena.

Trio.

PART II.

Concerto.

Aria.

Terzetto.

Cavatina.

Conductor, Mr. BALFE

PROGRAMME, PRINTED ON SATIN, OF THE BROMPTON HOSPITAL CONCERT.

given five times, though the season was nearly over, but it did not displace the old favourites, concerning which there is no more to be said. The Queen and Prince Albert continued to show their appreciation of Mlle. Lind to the end of the season, and Mr. Lumley had cause for satisfaction at the success of his two seasons with the singer, notwithstanding the fact that the result of the Bunn trial had been against him and had cost him £2,500.

During this second season Lumley had not only given his consent but also the use of Her Majesty's Theatre for a concert in aid of the Brompton Hospital for Consumption in which, as being near her little Clairville Cottage, Mlle. Lind was taking great interest at the time. Supported by her fellow-artists at the Opera, Mlle. Cruvelli, Messrs. Lablache, Gardoni and Belletti, with the addition of Mr. Otto Goldschmidt as pianist, and Mr. Balfe as conductor, a great concert was given, at raised prices, and a substantial sum realized. With it the hospital was enabled to build a much-needed new ward, and Mlle. Lind thus began the first of many contributions to public institutions in England.

Letters to her friends during this period show us what was in her mind during this busy season. She wrote to her Munich friend, Mme. Kaulbach:

LONDON, *July* 10, 1848.

DEAREST FRIEND.

It was very hard for me to take upon myself again this year the frightful responsibility of supporting the Opera here. But it was my duty to do so, as it rested with me whether Lumley should be ruined, and the whole theatre fall to the ground, or not; and the public rewards me in so many ways and shows me so many attentions that I have nothing to regret. I go this year also to the English provinces; but then I shall have done, and shall leave my "grande carrière" behind me, and shall only work in Sweden for my pleasure, that is, for my school.

There you have pretty well all that I shall undertake. If anything very important happens, I will be sure to tell you; but till then, believe nothing—and, before all things do not believe that I have a bad heart. I hope I have grown better; for, since I saw you, I have passed through many things, and have not been without temptations. What reason have I to be vain that I did not have before?

Your sincerely grateful friend,

JENNY LIND.

And again to her guardian:

CLAIRVILLE COTTAGE

Aug. 14, 1848.

I am going to sing a few more times this year, and therefore I shall not have done with London before the 20th inst. We go to the provinces on the 4th of September and begin at Birmingham on the 5th.

On my return to London I intend to give, in conjunction

with many others, a grand concert for the foundation of a school of music in memory of Mendelssohn, and we have chosen his last work *Elijah* to illustrate it. If this enterprise succeeds, I shall be very glad and happy. If I do not come home this autumn, I intend to work in Germany, for this purpose, part of the winter.

Mlle. Lind's "Tournée," as it was called, had been organized in advance by Lumley as part of the engagement for the season, and the boldness and sagacity of his calculations may be gauged by the fact, that though Mlle. Lind's fee was fixed at £10,000, he appears to have been very satisfied with his share of the profits.

The towns visited were Birmingham, Liverpool, Manchester, Hull, Newcastle, Edinburgh, Glasgow, Dublin, and Brighton, in all of which Mlle. Lind sang opera in her four chief rôles. She gave concerts in almost every place of importance, and worked without interruption till December 4, on which date, at Leeds, she gave a concert for the orchestra from which each man realized about £36; a nice wind-up for them to an agreeable and lucrative three months' work.

The entry in Mlle. Lind's engagement book of the performance of the *Figlia* at Brighton on November 3 is followed by eight notes of exclamation and has a thick line drawn beneath. I think we may safely assume that she intended this to be her last appearance on the stage. And so it would have been but for the six supplementary performances to be mentioned later.

Her stage triumphs did not represent the whole of her art life, and whatever her successes at Her Majesty's, the love that made her name a household word in English homes was won in the concert room, and in her oratorio singing. Not even the greatest Italian airs on the stage won the depth of affection that was given in an instant to the Swedish songs in the concert room. There were many other great artists and singers in her day, exciting admiration and gaining their triumphs, but Jenny Lind had a special niche of her own, by reason of her known simplicity of life and character and her great benevolence.

The death of Mendelssohn the previous year had been a great and abiding grief to her. His belief in her from the moment of their meeting had helped her to overcome her diffidence and to believe in herself, and it was through him that she came to find her truest happiness in oratorio singing, though he had not intended to influence her to leave the stage. On the contrary, he had been largely instrumental in finally inducing her to accept Lumley's London engagement. What more fitting way could there be therefore of collecting funds for his Memorial than by giving a performance of his last and greatest work, *Elijah*, in which he had really written the soprano part for Mlle. Lind, though she had not been able to come to England in time to sing it?

Mlle. Lind worked at her project all the autumn, invoking the help of her fellow-artists, who, like herself, gave their services gratuitously. With the exception of Herr Staudigl, and the substitution of herself in the soprano part, the artists were the same who had sung in the first original performance in Birmingham the previous year. A very fine interpretation of the oratorio, under the direction of Mr. Benedict, was ensured by careful rehearsing and much zeal, and a sum of close on £1,000 was the result. The sum, however, was insufficient in itself for the original plan, and a committee of prominent men in the musical world, with Sir George Smart at their head, undertook the management of the Fund and deemed it advisable to allow the sum to accumulate at interest until 1856, when Arthur Sullivan, then a Chapel Royal chorister, was elected to the first Travelling Scholarship in English musical education.

We may continue the history of the Mendelssohn

Scholarship by saying that in 1873 an appeal for funds added another £600 to the capital judiciously nursed by the committee, with Mr. Goldschmidt as the honorary secretary and sometime chairman, devoting much zeal to its welfare. The committee meets annually on November 4, the anniversary of Mendelssohn's death, and have so far elected sixteen scholars to this, the most coveted prize in the musical education of English men and women.

In addition to her artistic successes Mlle. Lind had also enjoyed many social ones and formed new friendships. One of these was exercising considerable influence in still more stiffening her distaste for the stage, though the influence was not to be of long duration. There had been no definite engagement for Mlle. Lind to sing for Lumley in the coming season but he hoped to persuade her to do so when the time came.

The season, however, opened without her, and the rival house triumphed; once more Lumley was threatened with disaster. To avert this Mlle. Lind offered the compromise of six performances of favourite operas to be given on the stage, but without action, or costume, or scenery. Such a compromise was foredoomed to failure, and only one performance took place; Mozart's *Flauto Magico* being given.

Mlle. Lind realized the mistake as well as anyone, and suspended her retirement from the stage for a few more performances. The house was once more filled to overflowing, but the pleasure of her re-appearance was tempered by the knowledge of its short duration.

The Queen and Court were present at Mlle. Lind's last appearance on any stage, which took place on May 10, 1849, when she played the same rôle of Alice in *Roberto* in which she had made her debut in London three seasons before. There were to be no "last nights" after the manner to which the theatre and concert public is accustomed, no supplementary performances, no "grand farewells." All who were present knew that Jenny Lind had really appeared on the stage for the last time when the curtain rang down on this occasion, after a scene of unbounded enthusiasm.

In this small book we have not even mentioned each rôle in which Mlle. Lind sang during her short operatic career. She only sang on the stage for eleven years, and out of the thirty operas of her repertoire few survive to-day. But in those eleven years Mlle. Lind had sung in opera 677 times, of which number 418 were sung in Stockholm, *and all this before her twenty-ninth year.*

LIST OF OPERAS

	Stockholm.	Berlin.	Vienna.	Munich.	Hanover.	Darmstadt.	Hamburg.	Copenhagen.	Frankfurt.	Stuttgart.	Carlsruhe.	Weimar.	Nuremburg.	Mannheim.	London.	English Provinces.	Edinburgh.	Glasgow.	Dublin.	Total.
La Sonnambula (Bellini)	28	11	7	2	–	1	9	–	4	1	1	1	1	–	22	6	1	1	2	98
Lucia di Lammermoor (Donizetti)	56	–	–	–	–	–	4	–	1	1	1	–	–	–	12	1	1	–	1	78
Norma (Bellini)	34	–	–	–	–	–	8	3	3	2	–	1	–	–	3	1	1	–	–	75
Roberto il Diavolo (Meyerbeer)	60	–	–	–	–	–	–	2	–	–	–	–	–	–	11	–	–	–	–	73
La Figlia del Reggimento (Donizetti)	18	2	6	3	–	–	4	2	–	1	–	–	1	1	17	4	–	1	2	62
Der Freischütz (Weber)	42	5	1	1	–	–	1	–	1	–	–	–	–	–	–	–	–	–	–	51
Divertissement National (Berwald)	27	–	–	–	–	–	–	–	–	–	–	–	–	–	–	–	–	–	–	27
Das Feldlager in Schlesien (Donizetti)	–	10	13	–	–	–	–	–	–	–	–	–	–	–	–	–	–	–	–	23
A May Day in Wärend (Berwald)	21	–	–	–	–	–	–	–	–	–	–	–	–	–	–	–	–	–	–	21
Die Zauberflöte (Mozart)	18	–	–	–	–	–	–	–	–	–	–	–	–	–	–	–	–	–	–	18
Il Don Giovanni (Mozart)	5	5	–	1	–	–	2	–	–	–	–	–	–	–	–	–	–	–	–	13
Le Nozze di Figaro (Mozart)	8	–	–	1	–	–	–	–	–	–	–	–	–	–	4	–	–	–	–	13
Marie (Herold)	11	–	–	–	–	–	–	–	–	–	–	–	–	–	–	–	–	–	–	11
La Vestale (Spontini)	6	3	–	–	–	–	–	–	–	–	1	–	–	–	–	–	–	–	–	10
Les Huguenots (Meyerbeer)	7	2	1	–	–	–	–	–	–	–	–	–	–	–	–	–	–	–	–	10
Die Schweizer Familie (Weigl)	10	–	–	–	–	–	–	–	–	–	–	–	–	–	–	–	–	–	–	10
Euryanthe (Weber)	5	4	–	–	–	–	–	–	–	–	–	–	–	–	–	–	–	–	–	9
La Straniera (Bellini)	9	–	–	–	–	–	–	–	–	–	–	–	–	–	–	–	–	–	–	9
Il Turco in Italia (Rossini)	9	–	–	–	–	–	–	–	–	–	–	–	–	–	–	–	–	–	–	9
L'Elisir d'Amore (Donizetti)	5	–	–	–	–	–	–	–	–	–	–	–	–	–	3	–	–	–	–	8
I Puritani (Bellini)	–	–	–	–	–	–	–	–	–	–	–	–	–	–	5	–	–	–	1	6
Ferdinand Cortez (Spontini)	6	–	–	–	–	–	–	–	–	–	–	–	–	–	–	–	–	–	–	6
Jag gor i Kloster (Berwald)	6	–	–	–	–	–	–	–	–	–	–	–	–	–	–	–	–	–	–	6
Le Château de Montenero (Dalayrac)	6	–	–	–	–	–	–	–	–	–	–	–	–	–	–	–	–	–	–	6
Armide (Gluck)	5	–	–	–	–	–	–	–	–	–	–	–	–	–	–	–	–	–	–	5
Anna Bolena (Donizetti)	5	–	–	–	–	–	–	–	–	–	–	–	–	–	–	–	–	–	–	5
La Gazza Ladra (Rossini)	4	–	–	–	–	–	–	–	–	–	–	–	–	–	–	–	–	–	–	4
I Masnadieri (Verdi)	–	–	–	–	–	–	–	–	–	–	–	–	–	–	4	–	–	–	–	4
The Elves (Van Boom)	4	–	–	–	–	–	–	–	–	–	–	–	–	–	–	–	–	–	–	4
Semiramide (Rossini)	3	–	–	–	–	–	–	–	–	–	–	–	–	–	–	–	–	–	–	3
Number of performances in each city	418	56	31	9	2	2	28	7	9	5	3	2	2	1	81	11	2	2	6	667

Total number of Operas: 30.

CHAPTER X

PUNCH AND JENNY LIND

IN Berlin and Vienna, as we have seen, the critics had written a great deal about Mlle. Lind, and in language which would seem very high-flown to us to-day. But those *critiques* are valuable as reflecting the high appreciation not only of her talent but of the earnestness of her nature and her art. Hans Andersen also has immortalized her in his story, "Das Märchen meines Lebens," and many a lesser poet made her the subject of his odes, which probably she never read. When she arrived in London, the leading journals there were also not slow to do the new singer full justice.

During the three seasons that Mlle. Lind sang at the Opera the various daily and weekly papers made constant and appreciative mention of her. The *Illustrated London News* had many pictures of her, and a final illustration of her going on board ship when she went to America. All these were seriatim accounts of her doings. But in *Punch* we have a fascinating and easy way of reading history "as she is felt," and the volumes for 1847–48–49 have innumerable mentions of Mlle. Lind both in verse and prose, of which we give a few examples:—*

"PUNCH'S" ODE TO THE SWEDISH NIGHTINGALE
(*From "Punch," Vol. XII*, 1847, *p.* 208.)

JENNY, before thy feet the dust I munch;
Despise me not, although there grows
Between my shoulders a prodigious hunch;
Because I have a crooked nose,
And in a head of monstrous size,
Carry a pair of goggle eyes;—
Yes, JENNY, thou hast fairly vanquish'd *Punch.*

Full many the warblers I have heard,
Whose song has won my approbation;
But still it always seemed to me absurd
To pay them aught like adoration;
For I esteem'd that it would be
Unworthy of my dignity
By that extreme emotion to be stirr'd.

But, JENNY LIND, I candidly avow
Thou hast bereft me of my wits;
Before thee I am not ashamed to bow.
What sparrows, wagtails, and tomtits,
To thee, sweet Nightingale of Sweden,
Meet songstress for the bowers of Eden,
Compared, appear all other song-birds now!

* By courtesy of the Proprietors of *Punch.*

It is not, Jenny, for thy peerless art,
That I adore thee—for the sake
Of sweetest pleasure which thy tones impart,
Or wondrous quaver, trill, or shake,
Nor yet because, with vocal strength,
Thou hold'st a note of certain length:
It is because thou singest to the heart.

And further, why thou charm'st this heart of wood,
Delightful Jenny, wouldst thou know?
Because thou look'st so gentle and so good,
And all accounts declare thee so;
Thy acting shows a sense of duty,
An earnest love of truth and beauty,
An aim to make thine author understood.

To thee should Genius, burning to outpour
Its lofty soul in song, intrust
Its inspirations; and once more
The mighty masters, laid in dust,
On earth appear; and Beethoven
Mozart, and Weber, come again,
And task for thee their spirits' richest lore.

Not oft I give a sentimental squeak,
Nor deal in homage; but thou hast,
Fair maid, drawn wooden tears down *Punch's* cheek,
And that is an achievement vast:
Thus, therefore, doth he bare his crown,
And throw him at thy footstool down,
Hoping that thou wilt smile on him this week.

The One Name before the Public

(*From "Punch," Vol. XII*, 1847, *p*. 220.)

Jenny Lind excites in the public mind an enthusiasm which now amounts to actual delirium, interrupted only by a few lucid intervals, when the attention is awakened by some very urgent necessity of life. In pity to her admirers, she should exert her powers of fascination less powerfully, for she is beginning to cause people to neglect their affairs, and leave the most important business unattended to.

Even in the Money Market, notwithstanding its tightness, it is common to hear Jenny Lind quoted instead of the rate of Exchange. Those who want their bills discounted ask you to cash them notes of Jenny Lind. The name of Lind is uttered when the proper word should have been Consols, scrip, or Venezuela bonds. It is to be feared that the "glorious simplicity of the Three per Cents." will soon be rendered one mass of confusion through being mixed up with Jenny Lind.

But if the City is wandering on the subject of Jenny Lind, the West End, as might be expected, is actually raving upon it. Ladies at Swan and Edgar's, speaking of a new silk, enquire, What is that Jenny Lind a yard? A gentleman, in presenting the object of his affections with a bouquet, begs that she will allow him to offer her a Jenny Lind; and a rose, it appears, will not only smell as sweet by this other name, but much sweeter. In the smoking-rooms at the Clubs, men talk of a prime cigar as a Jenny Lind, and request the pleasure of a glass of Jenny Lind with you, or desire you to pass the Jenny Lind this way. At all *conversaziones*, her name is mingled with the discussion; and but the other day, a lecturer at the Royal Institution, forgetting what he was about, said Jenny Lind when he meant hydrogen.

In short, the Swedish Nightingale has kindled a "blaze of triumph," which has produced the general effect of a *coup de soleil.*

Quite as Good as Money

(*From "Punch," Vol. XII,* 1847, *p.* 246.)

As there is a great scarcity of gold, we propose that some new scrip be issued, to be called the *Jenny Lind Scrip*. This might easily be managed, by allowing the tickets for the Italian Opera House to be received as a legal tender. Their value would of course depend upon the particular place to which the holder of the scrip would be entitled admission. A pit note would be less than one for the stalls, and a *coupon* for the boxes would be higher than either. This scrip has already been circulated to a very great extent in the Money Market, and in every instance has realised large sums. The holder of four Opera bonds for private boxes, with six *coupons* to each, cleared £100 last week.

The issue of gallery debentures also would rectify the evil in the same degree, though of course to a more moderate extent; for, being at a very high premium, they would supersede for a time the use of gold. We advise Ministers to be careful with the Exchequer Bonds, which only frighten people and agitate the market, and recommend them to purchase largely in the LUMLEY Funds, which is the great circulating medium at the present moment, and increase in value every day. If they do not do this rapidly, they may depend upon it the EMPEROR NICHOLAS will be before them in the Market and will be sending over some £5,000,000, or some such Russian trifle, to buy up as much JENNY LIND SCRIP as possible, as being the very best stock in Europe he can invest his money in. By the bye, there is a talk of a fresh issue of half-farthings. We are confident there is no demand for them, as long as there are so many English Opera-House debentures in the market.

"PUNCH'S" NATURAL HISTORY: THE SWEDISH NIGHTINGALE (*Curruca Lumlyana*).

(*From "Punch," Vol. XIV*, 1848, *p.* 197.)

THIS Nightingale is the most celebrated of all the warblers; but she is the one of which least need be said, simply because nothing can describe her. In the first place, there is no mistaking this Nightingale, nothing in the world singing like her. She is the most graceful of all the warblers, being about five feet high, with an extent and strength of wing that carry her over continents and across seas, borne upon the breath of heartiest, deepest gratitude and praise. Her shape is very succinct, and her habits at once frank, graceful, shy, and receding.

Her nest is in the wide world's heart, even though the said nest is feathered with the finest bank-paper, carrying the very heaviest figures.

She sings equally well whether by day or by night; and may often be heard in the vicinity of Hanover Square, about two in the afternoon; and as late as ten, somewhere in the Haymarket, in the evening.

Her range of voice is wonderful; reaching from the earth to the stars, whereabout she seems to flutter and dally,

"Still quiring to the young-eyed cherubim."

She does not deal in the "*jug-jug*" of the *Curruca luscinia*,—so well known to all pastoral folk, but gushes forth all sorts of sounds. Now we have—

"Oh, gioja, oh gioja,
Io ti ritrovo *Elvino*"

sounds that touch the tears into the eyes of the listener. And now she pours forth a stream of plaintive song, and our heart floats away upon it to blissfulness. Sometimes she pours out—

"Ah! Non giunge,"

and they seem to flash like a shower of diamonds, of ethereal sparks, kindling and subliming the sense they fall upon.

We cannot arrive at a certain knowledge of the food of this Nightingale. Some say she lives upon roses steeped in moonbeams; some, on melted amber. But, certain it is, from the divine emanations of her music, most certain it is—

"She on honeydew hath fed,
And drunk the milk of Paradise."

In fine, she is the Queen of Song, and as she lists, with her melodious lips controls each impulse of the subject heart.

THE NIGHTINGALE THAT SINGS IN THE WINTER

(*From "Punch," Vol. XVI*, 1849.)

WHEN the waters are stark, and the crystalline snow
Sparkles keen and unchanged in the morn's ruddy glow,
And the prism-coloured icicles flash in the sun,
The bitter cold stills all the song-birds but one.

Now the linnet, the lark, and the throstle are dumb,
E'en the stout little wren's gallant heart is o'ercome,
And the Nightingale, warbler so wondrous of tone,
That sings in the winter, is tuneful alone.

Sweetest creature, in song without rival or peer,
Far more inwardly vibrate thy notes than the ear,
For there speaks in that music, pure, gentle, refined,
The exquisite voice of a beautiful mind—

Of a spirit of earnestness, goodness and truth,
Of a heart full of tender compassion and ruth,
Ever ready to comfort, and succour, and bless,
In sorrow and suffering, in want and distress.

And the Nightingale's name by faint voices is praised,
For poverty aided, and Charities raised;
Not more good was the bird in whom childhood believes—
The Redbreast that cover'd the children with leaves.

And in tribute and love to a Memory revered,
By her magical voice noble monuments reared,
The high-minded communion with Genius attest,
Which gloriously thrills in the Nightingale's breast.

Now this Nightingale rare, in the winter who sings,
Being not yet a seraph, is one without wings;
And her name, which has travell'd as wide as the wind,
Is kind-hearted, generous, dear JENNY LIND.

After her decision to leave the stage became known Mr. Punch gave poor Bishop Stanley some serious words as to his supposed share in the decision. We who know how long her renunciation had been in her mind know that he had nothing to do with the inception of the idea, however he may have approved of the ultimate issue.

In the following week's edition Mr. Punch tackled Mlle. Lind herself, adducing among his arguments against her leaving the stage in the season of 1849 the loss to the theatre employees of their livelihood, which was the very reason why Mlle. Lind did appear again for a few more performances when she thought she had finished for all time.

Punch also gives an amusing duologue between Mlle. Lind and " Mr. Hare'sfoot," who pleads that his vocation is not wholly discreditable.

But we think that the full acknowledgment should be made of the gift of prophecy, when he already in 1849 suggested:

Music by Electric Telegraph

(*From "Punch," Vol. XVII, p.* 225, *Dec.* 15, 1849.)

It appears that songs and pieces of music are now sent from Boston to New York by Electric Telegraph. Our American brethren have among them such remarkable musical instruments, and in fact such astounding lyres, that nothing coming from the other side of the Atlantic can take us by surprise; and we are, therefore, not altogether dumbfounded by the announcement of music having been carried from one portion of the States to another on the wires of the Electric Telegraph. It must be delightful for a party at Boston to be enabled to call upon a gentleman in New York for a song.

The grand point of the invention, however, seems to be, that, if songs can be carried along the lines, our popular vocalists may treble or quintuple their present salaries, by singing in four or five places at once. Our own JENNY LIND, for example, who seems to be wanted everywhere at the same time, will have an opportunity of gratifying HER MAJESTY'S Theatre, and a couple of audiences, many hundred miles off, at the same moment. The telegraph, being found applicable for singing, may also be used by the shareholders who are beginning to sing pretty loudly for their dividends, as well as for the directors, who have been obliged to sing rather small during the last twelvemonth.

We hope the music of the wires may have the effect of restoring harmony to the railway world, which has long been out of tune, and which has lately been acting by no means in concert.

CHAPTER XI

HER ART AND PERSONALITY

AND here we want to dwell on the impression which Mlle. Lind's personality produced wherever she went. By nature she was highly strung and extremely diffident, and her upbringing had no doubt tended to make her reserved and sensitive, while preserving the simplicity of real genius.

It is a significant fact that in all her wanderings in the cities of Europe she was always to be found staying in the houses of interesting people, where the men were found forgathering with her and their wives mothering her.

Again, in her own city of Stockholm, where the circumstances of her young life might have stood in her way, she was everywhere welcomed in circles where birth and position are usually considered important, as well as in those other realms where only brains and character count. Her lofty ideals of an artistic mission and the consequent sense of responsibility carried her in dignified ease through the difficult surroundings of her youth while not detracting from her innate modesty.

In later years there was a sense of aloofness and almost haughtiness with those who were not her friends, this attitude giving offence to intruders on her private life whose visits she resented, and Mr. Goldschmidt had to use all his inherent powers of tact and diplomacy to put things right again.

Jenny Lind was undoubtedly born an artist, singing by instinct from her babyhood, and no doubt her histrionic gifts tended to her success in the first years of her Stockholm appearances, for her vocal methods were so far from perfect as to endanger her voice.

After her study with Garcia, Mlle. Lind's voice developed to a brilliant and powerful soprano, of beautiful quality and varying shades, and its compass extended from the B below the line to the G in the fourth line above it, that is to say, a clear two octaves and three-quarters.

SCALE OF JENNY LIND'S VOICE.

B below the line to G on the 4th line above it.

Her F sharp was so much admired that Mendelssohn

used it in "Hear ye, Israel," which he wrote for her, and later her husband used the same famous note in the air in his oratorio *Ruth*, also written for her.

The upper A is also prominently used in a syncopated passage of a cadence Mlle. Lind sang in *Casta Diva*, and again in one of her favourite Swedish melodies. The pianissimo rendering of these high notes was one of the most remarkable features of her singing. It was as rich in power as her mezzo-forte, and though falling on the ear like a whisper, reached the farthest corner of theatre or concert room. By nature her voice was not a flexible one; only perseverance and unremitting practice had made it so. Her breathing capacity was also not naturally great, but she renewed her breath so quietly and cleverly that the closest observer could not detect her doing it, and the outside world credited her with abnormal lung capacity. Her *messa di voce*, i.e. the art of swelling or diminishing her voice from the softest piano to the full volume of its power and vice versa was unrivalled by any singer. In like manner in her shakes, her scales, her legato, and staccato passages she evoked astonishment and admiration no less from competent judges than from the general public. And be it noted, the singer made use of ornaments and cadences only in so far as they were in perfect keeping with

Mon Abri
Cricklewood
Janvier 1895

Cher Mr Goldschmidt,

J'ai lu avec un vif intérêt les pages écrites par Mr Rockstro sous la forme descriptive, il donne une admirable leçon sur les difficultés que présente le chant et les procédés ingénieux employés par la Célèbre Cantatrice pour les dompter. Entre autres choses qu'il cite, on est frappé de l'adresse qu'elle déployait à respirer, du fini de son trille, de la tenue et de la justesse inébranlables de sa voix, soit dans la *messa di voce*, soit dans les traits d'agilité. Je me rappelle lui avoir entendu chanter dans le Messiah à Exeter Hall = Come unto me ye that labour" Les premières notes

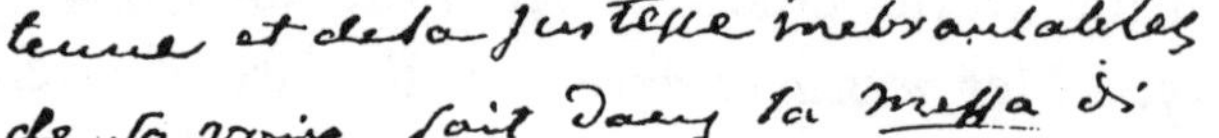
Come unto me all ye that la-bour

étaient si pleines, si pures, si justes que la ritournelle qui les précédait semblait fausse. Que l'on ajoute à ces qualités une immense tendresse qui dominait le morceau et on comprendra pourquoi l'irrésistible succès qui suivit le trille final, força la main même au rigide Costa.

J'aurais bien d'autres remarques à faire si j'entrais dans l'appréciation des points d'orgue et des exercices. Mais cher Monsieur Goldschmidt vous savez tout cela et mon effusion ne peut que vous dire quels sont mes sentiments d'admiration.

Au retour du beau temps, agréable de toutes manières, nous aurons, ma femme et moi, un grand plaisir à nous trouver dans votre compagnie, celle de votre famille et celle de vos amis.

Veuillez, je vous prie, offrir à Mme

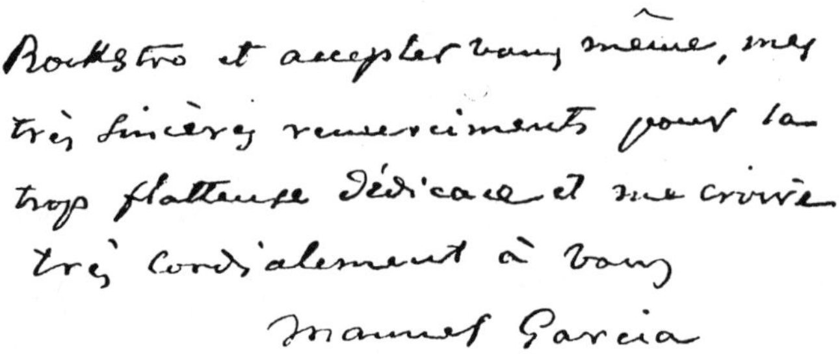
Rockstro et acceptez vous même, mes très sincères remerciments pour la trop flatteuse dédicace et me croire très cordialement à vous
Manuel Garcia

the intentions of the composer and the meaning o the music.

Messrs. Novello of Wardour Street publish a little book of Jenny Lind's method, together with a collection of her cadences, which were all of her own invention and had already been admired by Manuel Garcia when she studied with him in Paris. This book of "Methods and Cadences" was dedicated to Signor Garcia, then ninety years old, and he acknowledged a copy sent him in the accompanying letter, a translation of which is as follows:

MON ABRI,

CRICKLEWOOD, *Jan.* 1895.

DEAR MR. GOLDSCHMIDT,

I have been much interested in what Mr. Rockstro has written—he has given an admirable lesson on the difficulties of singing, and the ingenious methods with which the famous singer surmounted those difficulties. Among other things he cites, one is struck with the cleverness with which she managed her breathing, the finish of her shake, her hold over her voice, and its immutable purity of tone, whether singing *messa voce* or florid passages.

I remember hearing her sing in the *Messiah* at Exeter Hall. The first notes of "Come unto me, all ye that labour" were so full, pure, and perfect in intonation that the refrain which preceded them sounded out of tune. To these qualities there was added so much tenderness, in the singing of the whole air that one can understand that the irresistible applause which greeted the final shake, forced an encore from even the rigid Costa who was conducting.

I could say much more if I entered on the appreciation of her pauses (*points d'orgues*), and her exercises.

But, Dear Mr. Goldschmidt—you know all that, and my effusions can only prove to you my feelings of admiration.

etc. Yours very cordially,

M. G.

And this wonderful veteran only two years before had offered to teach Mme. Goldschmidt's grand-daughter when she should be a few years older!

In the course of her career Mlle. Lind's repertoire covered a wide range. With her abandonment of the stage at so early an age she was able to turn in her prime to the work of the giants in music. Having asserted her supremacy in the vocalization and interpretation of opera she now turned with all her intelligence to the study of Haydn, Handel, and Mozart, in whom many critics have considered her supreme, and the joy of her last years was in Bach's music. In lighter vein came her singing of the music of Mendelssohn and Schumann, inspired by the composers who were her friends.

It seems necessary, after having said this much about Mlle. Lind's voice and art, to give some account of her personal appearance, though words can convey little. Her features were strong and homely, of a usual Scandinavian type, but her mouth was very expressive and constantly changing with her emotions, so that while she sang one did not know or care whether she was beautiful or not, one only knew that she was great. Her eyes were grey-blue and her hair a *blonde cendrée* of very fine texture. At the time of her Swedish debut she wore the stiff ringlets which were the fashion of the day, but she very soon adopted the softer outline of her hair rolled over her ears and round her face, as shown in her numerous portraits, and this style she retained all her life.

Her height was 5 feet 5 inches, but she held her head so erect, and both walked and stood so well, that she appeared taller. She had well-moulded arms, neck, and shoulders, and well-shaped, if large, hands and feet. Her senses were very keen, particularly of smell, so that scents and tobacco fumes worried her, and she could not sing in a room in which were strong-smelling flowers.

As she had inherited the features of the Scandinavians, so she inherited also the strong feelings and undertone of melancholy which seems inseparable to those who love, as she did, the poetry of Sweden's woods and lakes, and these notes of pathos run through the national songs of which she was so great an interpreter. Few of Mlle. Lind's programmes failed to include songs by Lindblad, Kjerulf, Berg, or traditionals which are so attractive in their national feeling and simplicity. In Sweden she also sang songs written for her, words and music, by the historian, Geijer.

Nowadays letters are constantly cropping up which Jenny Lind wrote to her friends freely and intimately, and which now have passed to another generation. For in those days copious letter-writing was more usual than it is to-day. With her complete absence of conceit Mlle. Lind little thought that every scrap of her writing would be preserved, though her biographers have every reason to be glad that so many of her serious letters are available.

As to portraits, though there were many that are authentic, many more are reputed to be of her, where nothing except the style of hair-dressing and period of dress, recall the Mlle. Lind of those days.

Before closing this chapter, surveying briefly Mlle. Lind's character and attributes, we must touch on the deep religious feelings which largely shaped her life and motives. Imbued in her childhood with her grandmother's simple piety, she never wavered in her Lutheran creed. The Bible was her guide and stand-by, and she would have suffered acutely from the ideas of modern thought. All her life she was a regular church-goer, and indeed it is a fact that at her Malvern home the last time she ever went out was to take her eldest grandson to the Little Malvern church, and share her prayer-book with him, as was her custom.

As against her natural seriousness, she possessed a great fund of humour and joy in innocent gaiety ; and she was a splendid mimic, though careful in the use of that gift. She was very fond of dancing, but seldom allowed herself that pleasure for fear of over-taxing her strength and failing the public in her engagements. There are few, if any, instances of her having failed to keep one.

The question has often been asked why Jenny Lind left the stage when at the height of her fame. As we have seen, it was no sudden determination but a

Jenny Lind
Juli 1849

growing conviction that the life of stress and intrigue inseparable from the stage was contrary to her innermost nature and was playing havoc not only with her peace of mind but also with her physical powers. We must remember how early she had begun a strenuous life and how alone she stood, not only in family but in business matters. With her idealistic and religious temperament it was difficult to endure the fret, worry, and jealousies of a theatrical life, and, as we have seen in the Bunn affair, she was liable to rush into a business which gave her subsequent trouble. It was unnatural for a young woman, who was first and foremost an artist, to have to battle with commercialism and dwell in an unsympathetic atmosphere whilst secretly craving for the security of a fixed home and family life.

No one can have read this story so far without realizing that Mlle. Lind's character was one of great simplicity, entirely free of feminine wiles, and that "love-affairs" had no part in her life. We have already quoted a letter from her to Mme. Erichsen in which she deplored having to battle with life alone and in a crowd, and for some years she had thought to end the loneliness and battling in a companionable marriage with a fellow-artist on the Swedish stage. But after entering on her wider European experiences, and with her decision to leave the stage, to which he still belonged, the engagement lapsed by mutual consent.

With her now avowed affection for England and the English, at the close of her 1849 season, Mlle. Lind once more entered on a project of marriage, this time with a young Englishman, and the last weeks of her stay in England were clouded by indecision. There was much in common between the two, particularly in matters of religion, but the rock they foundered on was that, while admiring her personally, he and his family disapproved of the stage and its traditions which had made her great, and she felt that such an attitude constituted a slur on her whole former life. Moreover, the narrowness of outlook and want of freedom in the proposed alliance frightened the woman and clashed with the instincts of the artist. Once more she was in doubts and difficulties and took refuge in flight to friends in Paris, there to recover from the pain the decision had cost her.

But even to Mlle. Lind's perturbed mind Paris at its best in the month of May, and the company of many intimate friends, must have offered consolation, and her old self gradually came back to her. She appears to have called on Meyerbeer and busied herself in giving a singing lesson to a young Swede each morning. She also sang at the Swedish Minister's, and at another house, in private. But she received a terrible shock in the sudden death from cholera of Mme. Catalani, to whom she had been singing only two days before. The whole party thereupon left Paris and some of them (including Judge Munthe, who had gone to Paris to advise her on many matters) journeyed to Brussels and the Rhine. But doctors were now insistent that the state of her nerves and her constant headaches demanded a long rest, and she therefore wandered at her ease in the Tyrol and South Germany for some months, though letters were following her with offers of engagements from many parts of the globe, including America.

During this time Mlle. Lind was, as usual, writing freely to her friends Mme. Wichmann and Mme. Birch-Pfeiffer, and from Schlangenbad she apparently wrote to Mme. Mendelssohn for the first time since her husband's death. In her letter she apologizes for her long silence and for reopening a wound which will never close. In this letter she breaks out about his *Elijah*, which she calls "sublime."

In my opinion he never wrote anything finer; and could not have written anything loftier in the future. With what solemnity we all stood there to perform it, and with what love do people still speak of him. How the good English have understood and absorbed this particular music! As for myself, I sing it in quite a special mood. . . . You cannot but be grateful when you consider how much, and in what a lofty manner, you were esteemed and loved by a being, not only exceptionally endowed, but pure and original as he was! . . . God be with you, beloved lady, and do not forget,

Your sincerely loving,

JENNY LIND.

Mlle. Lind sang at several concerts during this November and December in Hamburg, and one of these was given, with full orchestra, by Mr. Otto Goldschmidt, of whom she saw a good deal in these days. They did much music together, Mendelssohn being a common bond between them, and Mr. Goldschmidt began to persuade her to sing again those songs of Mendelssohn, which for two years since his death she had not had the courage to attempt.

CHAPTER XII

1849–1850

MLLE. LIND was at Lübeck when the project of the American tour really took shape. She then had Mlle. Åhmanssohn with her, who had replaced Louise Johannsen as her companion, and she was contemplating a tour in Russia, as she needed money. Not for herself, as her wants were few, but for her schemes for home charities. A new proposal, however, ousted the Russian plan; a proposal for a great American tour, with Mr. Barnum as her impresario. That astute gentleman had sent his agent, Mr. Wilton, who placed himself steadily by her side and pressed for an answer to Mr. Barnum's offer.

The idea of an American tour had been suggested before, but there was more than suggestion in Mr. Barnum's methods, and he offered her the fulfilment of her dreams of charitable enterprises and immunity from financial anxieties in the future. With no one but Mlle. Åhmanssohn to consult, Mlle. Lind, usually so mistrustful of her own judgment, signed the contract, and herself conducted the correspondence with Baring Brothers, as to Barnum's stability and financial position.

Mr. Barnum understood the conditions of his day. He had before now provided food for the gaze of blind wonder; he was now to bring to Americans the splendid satisfaction of hearing the voice of Jenny Lind. From first to last he treated her well and generously, and remained her firm friend long after his business relations ceased.

The contract was for one hundred and fifty concerts in the space of one year or eighteen months, counting the day of her arrival in New York, but leaving her full power to decide as to the number of concerts in one week, as well as the number of pieces she would sing at each concert; not fewer than two concerts a week, or four pieces at each concert. Everything was to be regulated with due regard for her health and voice.

In consideration of these services Mlle. Lind was to have all expenses of travelling and hotels paid for herself, her lady companion, and a secretary; in addition she was to be given a maid and a manservant and a carriage and pair. Her fee was to be £200 for every concert at which she sang.

There was a notable stipulation that Mlle. Lind should have perfect freedom to sing for charitable purposes whenever she wished to do so, only consulting Mr. Barnum as to their mutual convenience, and nowhere singing for charity until after two concerts had been given in that place, under her contract with him. Finally she pledged herself to start for America by the last boat in August or the first in September. So, roughly, ran the contract, signed and sealed on January 9, 1850.

After the contract was settled Mlle. Lind remained some time in Lübeck in a frame of mind full of contentment and with the knowledge that the peace she had secured by her abandonment of the stage was not at the cost of further opportunities for the exercise of her art. A career was assured to her in the concert room which would fulfil her aims. Nothing she valued was lost, while much that she detested was thrown aside.

She wrote details of her plans to her friend Baroness French in Florence and to Mme. Wichmann in Berlin, and said how relieved she was at having secured her life for the next two years. She told them she liked Mr. Benedict, who was to go with her as pianist, accompanist, and conductor, and her old friend Signor Belletti was also to be of the party. In other letters she was writing of a Christmas-tree which she had thoroughly enjoyed and of a children's ball she was to give on January 17. Serious as she mostly was, Mlle. Lind could also at times enjoy a gaiety that was infectious, and no wonder that she managed to make the Lübeck hotel merry. Perhaps it may have added to the pleasure of her ball that young Mr. Otto Goldschmidt had come over from Hamburg and danced with her several times!

The finale of her last English visit still haunted her painfully, but the American tour offered an escape from recent troubles and uncertainties, and in the meantime she was pleasantly engaged in a series of concerts in North Germany.

On January 20 Mlle. Lind sang at Hanover once more, and was again most kindly received by the Royal family, who had heard her in operatic rôles on her previous visit. They now fully appreciated her concert performances, and especially delighted in her singing of Swedish melodies.

From Hanover Mlle. Lind went to Göttingen, where she gave two concerts, one for her own benefit and one for charity, when the students were swept in to a storm of enthusiasm over her rendering of Mendelssohn's *Rheinisches Volkslied*. In it the F sharps that frequently occur lent themselves to the most enthralling powers of her voice, and it is no wonder that the students lost their heads that evening. They made her a Sister Associate of their Hannovera Corps and presented her with their corps ribbon inscribed with their thirty-two names. In her letter of thanks Mlle. Lind said she regarded the gift with joy and pride and would keep it to her dying day, which was no idle word, for it is still treasured in the family.

After another concert in Hanover and others at Oldenburg, Bremen, and Brunswick, Mlle. Lind passed on to her familiar quarters with the Wichmanns in Berlin, and sang several times, chiefly for charity. She wrote a simple account of her doings to Judge Munthe: "What a joy it is to see the people so satisfied! Always crowded houses, and I have got together quite a lot for the poor by my singing these last weeks. Praise be to God!"

Mlle. Lind was singing the airs from the *Puritani*, *Turco in Italia*, and Meyerbeer's duet *La Grandmère* with Mlle. Tuczec; also Schumann's *Sonnenschein*, Lindblad's *Schlottfegerbub*, and Taubert's *Ich muss nun einmal singen*. The Berliners took great pride in the fact that theirs was the first town in which she had sung in opera when at last she had been induced to sing out of Sweden.

On March 20 Mlle. Lind travelled to Hamburg, where she surprised the Schumanns by arriving in time to sing at a concert they were giving. Mme. Schumann in her diary gives an affectionate picture of her appearance and how she sang. At the soirée Schumann remarked after she had sung his *Sonnenschein*, "That really does put the sun on one's back," and she put all her soul into "*Der Himmel hat eine Thräne geweint*," which ever remained one of the most touching songs among the many that she sang in after life. Mme. Schumann also told how Mlle. Lind sang many of Schumann's songs at sight, in such a manner that the composer felt as if she had sung them straight out of his heart.

On her return to Lübeck, bad weather in the Baltic delayed her journey to Sweden, and she took advantage of it to give three charity concerts in Lübeck, one for the poor of that town, one for the widow of the conductor Bach, and one for the pianist Schreinzer.

In a letter to her friend Mrs. Salis Schwabe, in Manchester, she tells of her doings and how she enjoys singing to the Germans, who are so alive to music. She is impatient to see the Atlantic and America and Niagara, and fears she will have little time to stay in her beloved England on her way to

Liverpool. She says that her voice is in good order, and her headaches less violent. She again mentions Mr. Otto Goldschmidt and his having danced with her, as well as played in a concert, and enjoyed a little spring air !

She reached Stockholm once more on the *Gauthiod* on May 12 and was welcomed by an enormous crowd on the quay. She was to sing by Royal command at six concerts at the Royal Theatre, since the King respected her decision to quit the stage, and besides, there were to be two State concerts during June in honour of the marriage of the Crown Prince. The tickets for the public concerts were put up to auction and all the profits were taken by the theatre. Mlle. Lind's fees of 1,000 kroner (£30) were given by her to the Employees' Fund.

Though no longer appearing in costume parts, the Swedes were as enthusiastic as ever over her singing of the old operatic airs. Her friend Mlle. de Stedingk warmly defended her resolution to leave the stage, and wrote in her diary: "Many people blame her ; but I cannot possibly do so as I know the convictions on which she bases her decision. She now only sings in concerts, and has deliberately renounced the triumphs and admiration she everywhere excites, and this for a resolution which makes her more worthy of honour than ever. Many people suppose her decision is from pious motives, but that is not the case. Jenny Lind is as God-fearing as pure, but had piety been the cause she would not herself go to plays to see others act, which she enjoys! She feels how morally and physically wearing is the work in the service of dramatic art, so that for days after a performance of *Norma* her nerves are too shattered for either useful or mental occupation."

After one of the Court soirées the Queen offered Mlle. Lind a diamond bracelet, which she begged to be allowed to decline, asking only for a little bunch of forget-me-nots out of a vase on the table. This is one of many similar incidents.

In the month of June, however, she was bound to accept a gratifying tribute from the lovers of music in the whole of Sweden. This took the form of a medal, struck with her portrait on the face, and symbolic figures and an inscription on the reverse. It was cast in gold, silver, and bronze, and the gift was accompanied by an address in graceful language signed by a long list of subscribers headed by the King. Those medals were cherished by her all her life and bequeathed to the Stockholm National Museum at her death.

Before leaving Stockholm Mlle. Lind sang

programmes of sacred music in two churches, the *Elijah* air, " Then shall the righteous shine forth," being one item. One of the churches was Santa Clara, in the parish of which she was born, and here it was on June 25 that she sang in Sweden for the last time in her maiden name.

CHAPTER XIII

1850–1852

MLLE. LIND left her country with a happy sense of the goodwill that was following her career, and she fulfilled a few engagements on her way across Europe before joining her companions Messrs. Benedict and Belletti, in London. After a few days' stay there she journeyed to the home at Manchester of her friends the Salis Schwabes, in order to rest a few days before singing in Liverpool on August 16 and 17. The two concerts were to raise funds towards paying for the new hall of the Liverpool Philharmonic Society. At the first concert she sang the airs "*Qui la voce*," "*Non paventar*," a duet with Belletti, a new song of Benedict's called "Take this lute," and, finally, the "Echo Song" to her own accompaniment. This was all old ground, but at the second concert Mlle. Lind made a vital new departure, for it was the first time that she sang the *Messiah*, in which in later years she proved herself incomparable.

The well-known *Times* critic of those days, Mr. Davison, reported as to the excitement and curiosity prevailing about the performance, mobs besieging the hall during rehearsal in the hope of getting a glimpse of the singer. He warmly commends her as being the first to arrive and the last to leave the rehearsal, to which she gave all her attention. As to the performance, he wrote that Mlle. Lind's singing surpassed anticipation and enhanced her reputation, and paid tribute to the simplicity with which she sang "He shall feed His flock," as well as drawing attention to the devotion in the airs "How beautiful are the feet" and "I know that my Redeemer liveth." Be it noted here that in this last air Mlle. Lind always put the accent as almost a confession of faith on the word *know*. Mr. Davison wound up by describing the extraordinary enthusiasm after Mlle. Lind had sung the principal verses of the National Anthem, and said: "It was a leave-taking such as even Jenny Lind had rarely experienced."

It was a wonderful transition from the atmosphere of the Italian Opera to that of the English concert platform, but her hearers now knew that her gifts were supreme in both branches of her art. They heartily welcomed her on the new ground of oratorio, and it was to the English that she especially loved to sing that music.

Mlle. Lind's last day at Liverpool was occupied in visiting the new wing of the Southern and Toxteth Hospital, to the building of which she had materially helped by her concert of the previous year, and on this occasion she was presented with some beautiful silver as a memento of her help.

The *Illustrated London News* of August 24 gave an account of the popular excitement over her embarkation on the steamer *Atlantic*, and the police had advised Barnum's agent to get her on board before the expected hour, so that the excited crowds that lined the shore had to content themselves with a sight of the little lady waving her handkerchief from the paddle-box as the boat steamed away.

Such was the farewell of the artist leaving the triumphs of the Old World for the uncertainties of the New. But she was not long in doubt. In her innocence she had known nothing of the drum-beating and nursed excitement by which Mr. Barnum was stirring the American public to bless his venture and greet the new arrival, and we must bear in mind the fact that at this time Mlle. Lind's name and fame were comparatively unknown on that side of the water, and Mr. Barnum was risking an enormous sum on his faith in the singer. Under his agreement he had to place in advance, 187,500 dollars with the London bankers, and in order to do so he had to collect all his funds, and still was short of the amount. He eventually raised the required sum, though Wall Street had told him that he would never take more than 3,000 dollars at any concert, and would be beggared by the venture!

The contract had been signed, as we have said, at Lübeck in January of the year, and soon afterwards Mr. Barnum began to prepare the public mind.

In a letter to the Press of February 22 he began by reciting that even if he lost by the enterprise he would be proud to have been instrumental in introducing to the States a lady whose vocal powers were unique and whose character was goodness, simplicity, and charity personified. He said that Mlle. Lind was anxious to visit America, of whose institutions she had heard so much. In her tour, which included Havana, she had the right to give charitable concerts whenever she thought proper, and he finally mentioned the fact that from her earnings she had already given away more than the whole amount which Mr. Barnum was going to pay her.

In his own account of this venture of his, Mr. Barnum has said that though he relied on Mlle. Lind's great reputation as an artist, he also largely estimated her success with all classes of the American public on account of the interest aroused by her extraordinary benevolence and generosity.

Much the same scenes were enacted on Mlle. Lind's arrival as had speeded her parting from Liverpool, and on their first meeting Mlle. Lind was astounded to find that Mr. Barnum had never heard her sing! He said that he had relied on her reputation, which he rated higher than his own judgment in musical matters. From the ship to the Irving House, where her apartments were to be, Mr. Barnum must be pardoned if he took his seat by the driver of the carriage as a legitimate sign of victory, and on such an advertisement within ten minutes of their arrival Broadway was congested with thousands of eager sightseers.

This is how *Punch* (Vol. XIX, 1850, p. 146) told London of what he thought was going on across the water: *

JENNY LIND AND THE AMERICANS.

From our own Reporters.

THE moment it was known by what vessel JENNY LIND was about to cross the Atlantic, we dispatched an efficient corps of reporters and correspondents on board, who were present

* By courtesy of the proprietors of *Punch.*

in various disguises about the ship, for the purpose of watching every movement of the Nightingale. One of our most esteemed contributors might have been seen flitting about in a dreadnought and sou'-wester, from spar to spar, and yard-arm to yard-arm, dodging the delicious song-bird, as

CORONATION OF JENNY THE FIRST—QUEEN OF THE AMERICANS.

she hopped from paddle-box to paddle-box, utterly regardless of wind and wave, while a juvenile member of our extensive establishment was on board, in the humble disguise of a lob-lolli-boy.

It has been erroneously supposed, that because MADEMOISELLE JENNY LIND was seen to leave Liverpool waving her white handkerchief from the very top of the deck-house over the companion, and was seen to enter the American harbour from the top of the same deck-house,—it has been, we say, erroneously, though naturally supposed, that, from the time of her starting to the moment of her arrival, JENNY LIND was constantly employed in the way in which she is represented to have commenced and terminated her journey. We are enabled to assure the public, on the very best authority, that such is not the case.

The time occupied in the voyage passed very pleasantly. Every evening there was a concert for the benefit of somebody or other, concluding with one for the benefit of the crew, which was somewhat marred by the boisterous state of the weather. The piano was soon sent up to an inconveniently high pitch, the glasses insisted in joining in, as musical glasses without much regard to harmony or effect, but keeping up a sort of jingle during the whole time, there was an occasional accompaniment of wind and stringed instruments by BOREAS playing fearfully on the ropes of the rigging, and every now and then everything was rendered a great deal too flat by a too rapid running up of the ascending scale and coming very abruptly down again.

The voyage having been safely got over, we now come to the proceedings in America; but we are bound to say that our contemporaries have so fully occupied the ground —and their own columns—that room is scarcely left even for us to say anything.

For some days before the steamer was expected, New York was in a state of intense excitement, so that when the ship actually came in sight, the only mode the police had of keeping the enthusiasm of the crowd within decent bounds, was to check their cries by knocking the breath— as far as practicable—out of their bodies. Millions had their heads turned, and hundreds had their heads broken, but all was of no avail; and in spite of the exertions of the constabulary to stave off the people with their staves, the quays were in a state of deadlock from the throngs that covered them. As the vessel entered the harbour, the Nightingale was seen perched on the deck-house, supported on either side by MESSRS. BENEDICT and BELLETTI. MR. BARNUM, the enterprising showman who has speculated in JENNY LIND, as he has already done in TOM THUMB, and other popular idols, was running a race along the pier with a MR. COLLINS—perhaps a rival showman—each holding an enormous bouquet, and a fearful struggle took place as to which should be the first to clamber up the paddle-box. BARNUM made a desperate spring on one side, while COLLINS took a terrific leap towards the other, and the latter being the more fortunate, or the more active of the two—or perhaps he had been taking lessons in gymnastics beforehand of some Indian-rubber brothers—succeeded in being the first to stand at the Nightingale's side, and to present her with a nosegay twice the size of that which BARNUM pushed into her hand a moment afterwards.

Either to see better, or to escape from the energetic COLLINS and the frantic BARNUM, "JENNY LIND moved to the larboard wheel-house," and seeing the American flag, the Nightingale—with a sly sense of humour, no doubt, and a general recollection of all that she had heard about the slave-trade, and the treatment of MR. FREDERIC DOUGLAS, the "coloured" newspaper editor—exclaimed, "There is the beautiful standard of freedom, the oppressed of all nations worship it."

As the ship neared the pier, every mast seemed to be

made of eyes, noses, and mouths; every window was a mass of heads; and the roofs of the houses looked as if they were slated with human beings, and had men and women for chimney-pots. The Nightingale was so struck with the respectability of a Yankee mob, that she asked "where the poor were?"—intending, no doubt, if there had been any poor, to have sung at once—sung out from the top of the paddle-box—for their benefit.

It now became time for JENNY LIND to land, and at the pier gates was drawn up in readiness BARNUM's carriage. When one hears of a showman's carriage in this country one's mind naturally travels to a van into which the public are invited, indiscriminately, to "walk up"; but such was not the vehicle in which BARNUM was prepared to receive his Nightingale. The horses were figged out in a style well adapted to advertise the museum of which BARNUM is proprietor; and, though the trappings were well calculated to act as trappings, and catch the eye of the vulgar, good taste could not help feeling that the "caparisons" were "odious." The Nightingale entered the carriage with the assistance of BARNUM, who then mounted the box, ordering his servant to make a circuit towards Irving House, it being very clear to all what he and his coachman were driving at. The progress to Irving House was one tremendous crush of beings, so densely packed together that an exceedingly ripe cheese, in spontaneous motion, is the only thing to which it would bear comparison.

The Times, having devoted a first leader of nearly three columns to a digest of the proceedings—including the telegraphing of MRS. and MISS BARNUM, who were coming up from Cincinnati, the rush of Bishops and Clergy, the crowd of "fashionable ladies," the deadly scramble for the stone of the "identical peach," supposed to have been eaten by JENNY LIND at dessert, the search for a "sensible old horse," who must be a rare animal among the tribe of senseless donkies in the States—these things, we say, having been sufficiently dwelt upon elsewhere, we think reiteration of the facts would be superfluous. We are, however, expecting to receive telegraphic dispatches of a somewhat startling character, nor should we be surprised if the next "Latest from America" should announce the dissolution of the Republic, and the proclamation of JENNY LIND as Queen of the United States, with BARNUM as chief Secretary for Foreign Affairs—a post for which his long acquaintance with such foreign affairs as TOM THUMB, the Sea Serpent, and other contents of his museum, renders him fully qualified.

Our anticipations are realised, the following is the

LATEST FROM AMERICA—JENNY LIND.

BY ELECTRIC TELEGRAPH.

Mr. Punch's Office, 85, *Fleet Street.*

Within a minute of going to press, we have received the following important intelligence from Liverpool:—

"The *Tarnation*, CAPTAIN SMART, has just arrived from New York, after five days' passage, and brings the following authentic information.

"JENNY LIND does not return to Europe. On the conclusion of her engagement (which will be considerably shortened) with BARNUM, JENNY will be crowned Queen of the United States, the actual President politely retiring. JENNY accepts office under contract always to sing in so many airs, to the people of the smartest nation upon earth, what has hitherto been printed as Presidents' Speeches.

"Two stars and one stripe have been added to the American flag: the stars are JENNY's eyes, and the stripe a lock of JENNY's hair."

We can only give the merest sketch of the weeks of excitement that followed Mlle. Lind's arrival, and resulted in the crowding out of every concert that she gave.

Mr. Barnum had given a prize of 200 dollars for an ode, "Greeting to America," which Mlle. Lind sang at her first concert at Castle Garden, New York, on September 11, 1850. The full programme is as follows:

PROGRAMME OF MLLE. LIND'S FIRST CONCERT IN AMERICA.

CASTLE GARDEN, NEW YORK, 11TH SEPTEMBER, 1850.

GRAND OVERTURE, *Oberon* . . . . . *Weber*

AIR from *Maometto* . . . . . . *Rossini*
SIGNOR BELLETTI.

Casta Diva . . . . *Bellini*
MLLE. LIND.

GRAND DUET FOR PIANOFORTE . . . *Airs by Bellini*
MESSRS. BENEDICT AND HOFFMAN.

Turco in Italia . . . . *Rossini*

DUET, MLLE. LIND AND SIGNOR BELLETTI.

ORCHESTRAL OVERTURE, "The Crusaders" . *Benedict*

TRIO from *The Camp of Silesia* . . . *Meyerbeer*

MLLE. LIND and Flautists.
(MESSRS. KYLE AND SIEDE.)

Largo al Factotum . . . . *Mozart*

SIGNOR BELLETTI.

"Herdsman's Song" (Known as "The Echo Song") . . . . *Swedish Melody*

MLLE. LIND.

"Greeting to America," words by Bayard Taylor *Benedict*

MLLE. LIND.

In the last item but one it is amusing to find a confusion unnoticed till this day. For the famous "Echo Song" is a Norwegian melody, and the "Herdsman's Song" was written by Mlle. Lind's singing master, Berg. Both these songs were constantly sung by Mlle. Lind. Mr. Barnum, probably, at that date did not know the difference, and Mlle. Lind is not likely to have seen the proofs of the programme.

Mlle. Lind's own impressions are contained in a letter written from Boston to her parents in the little home she had given them in Sweden. It is dated September 27, 1850. After describing the voyage as having been very interesting, with variations of storm, fog, and calm, and lasting eleven days, during which she was never seasick, she goes on to say:

I have met with quite an astonishing reception and have given, already six concerts in New York, in a hall that holds 11,000 people. It has been crowded each time, and we shall be able, most likely to give 40 or 50 concerts in New York alone. Here everything is done on a large scale. The first ticket sold here (Boston) for to-day's concert was sold by auction for as much as 625 dollars! It is amazing what heaps of money they seem to have here. My health, thank God, is excellent and my voice fresh and strong, and I am looking forward, when this tournée is over to a time of peace and rest. For indeed, in these two matters so precious to human beings, I seem to be given little share, torn and bothered as I am from morning to night. Still it is touching to see how much good-will and kindness I receive; people seem not to know how, enough, to show their favour and genuine interest. I wish I could send home to you some of the lovely fruit and flowers I continually receive. We have lovely warm weather, still, and ever a divinely blue sky. Time does pass; I shall soon be 30 years of age. How happy I am to become "an ould hag"! Every day I see round me numbers of new faces and I find it rather a bore, but I am trying to terminate my engagement perhaps in a year. When we meet I shall have heaps to relate which I have now no time for.

It is already more than 3 months since I was dancing round the May-pole at home. Now pray take care of yourselves, and remember with tenderness your far-off daughter.

It is rather sad to think that Mme. Lind did not live to see her daughter again, or to enjoy for longer the softening influences of a happier existence, free from care.

Mlle. Lind was also writing to Judge Munthe at the same time. She tells him that she has given eight concerts with great success. She devoted the first two in New York to charity, because they had raised such enormous sums by auctioning the tickets. She tells him that her agreement with Barnum has been quite altered, and he is showing himself extremely generous and reasonable. The receipts are never less than 10,000 dollars and vary between 12,000, 14,000, and 16,000, so that her share for six concerts is about 30,000 dollars.

And yet with all this turmoil she lived her own quiet inner life, waiting only for the moment of release, as she had told her parents.

We cannot follow Mlle. Lind in detail through her 137 concerts in thirty-seven different towns, but a few of them deserve brief details. At her concert at Boston on October 10 she sang for the first time in America the air from the *Elijah*, "If with all your hearts," which is of course a tenor air, but Mlle. Lind was very fond of singing it. For the first time in America at this concert she sang Weber's "*Und ob die Wolke*" from *Der Freischütz*, a *Sonnambula* air, and two Swedish songs. The full programme is as follows:

TREMONT TEMPLE, BOSTON, OCTOBER 10, 1850.
(For Charity.)

OVERTURE to *Egmont* . . . . . . *Beethoven*
By the Orchestra.

"If with all your hearts" (from the *Elijah*) *Mendelssohn*
MLLE. LIND.
(First time in America.)

"Non piu andrai" . . . . . . *Mozart*
SIGNOR BELLETTI.

SONGS without words . . . . . *Mendelssohn*
MR. BENEDICT.

"Und ob die Wolke" (from the *Freischütz*) . *Weber*
MLLE. LIND.
(First time in America.)

PART II

"Die Felsen Mühle" . . . . . *Reissiger*
By the Orchestra.

"Piff Paff" (*Huguenots*) . . . . . *Meyerbeer*
SIGNOR BELLETTI.

"Come per me sereno" (*Sonnambula*) . . *Bellini*
MLLE. LIND.
(First time in America.)

"Miei rampolli" . . . . *Rossini*

SIGNOR BELLETTI.

"Och hör du lilla flicka" . . . *Dalecarlian Melody*

"Fjeran i skug" . . . . . . *Berg*

MLLE. LIND.

(Both for the first time in America.)

As instancing her dislike of raised prices of tickets we find at the foot of this programme the notice that she would give two concerts at reduced prices "in order to give all who wish to hear Mlle. Lind the opportunity to do so."

Mlle. Lind always desired to reach the place where she was to sing without having her arrival known, and this was rather a problem to her impresario, who preferred the excitement of publicity as aid to advertisement.

At Washington, President Fillmore called on Miss Lind, and she and her party spent some pleasant hours in the private circle of the President's family, who attended both of her concerts, as did every member of his Cabinet. Mr. Webster had been introduced to her in Boston, and we hope the story is true that on her having at his request sung the Swedish "Echo Song" he rose from his seat and made her a profound bow when she had finished. The voyage from

Wilmington to Charleston was so perilous and protracted that it took thirty-six instead of the usual seventeen hours. Mlle. Lind, as we have seen on the Atlantic voyage, was a good sailor, but the feared loss of the steamer had been telegraphed to the northern cities of America with much concern. At Charleston the party rested and spent Christmas, always an important event for Mlle. Lind, and she celebrated it with a tree and surprises and jokes for all, her present to Mr. Barnum being a little statuette of Bacchus as a hit at his temperance principles!

Though Mr. Barnum had taken much trouble about quarters, at Havana, they were not a success, and on the first day Mlle. Lind disappeared in a *volante* with an interpreter on the box, to return triumphant at having rented a commodious house outside the town, to which she invited all the others to stay with her. Frederica Bremer spent a few days very pleasantly there too, and perhaps it was on this occasion that she considered Mlle. Lind's cheeks required the improvement of the packet of rouge with which she presented her. But it never was used, and was found endorsed, among Mme. Goldschmidt's relics. The period of rest and sunshine in Mlle. Lind's house was altogether delightful, for she was free from intruders and her time was her own.

The people of Havana, however, were in an angry mood, being unaccustomed to the high-priced tickets that had obtained in the States, and they were not disposed to welcome the singer amiably. In spite of this they attended the first concert in fair numbers, and this wholly new attitude was met by Mlle. Lind with splendid courage.

The *New York Tribune* described how when Mlle. Lind was led on to the platform by Signor Belletti, at once a storm of hisses drowned the few hand-claps. At all times Mlle. Lind was nervous at the opening of her concerts, and there was the usual tremulousness on this occasion. But when she realized the difference of reception from that to which she was accustomed, her courage blazed forth into a haughty bearing, her eyes flashed defiance, and she stood immovable as a statue, ready to fight a battle and win. Some of the old Castilians kept a frown on their faces, but their ladies and most of the audience looked surprised as the tones of that voice flowed on in increasing meaning and beauty, till its power broke down all opposition and she was acclaimed again and again. We do not blame Mr. Barnum for refusing to give more than the advertised four concerts, the fourth being for charity.

After this pleasant month's rest the party crossed

to New Orleans, once more to encounter busy scenes. The whole of February was spent at New Orleans, where thirteen concerts were given, the last for charity, and then the party boarded the Mississippi steamer *Magnolia*, making arrangements with the captain to delay sufficiently at four towns on the river, for a concert to be given in each. Mlle. Lind sang without ceremony in the ship's saloon for the pleasure of the passengers. The concert at Memphis was the sixtieth on the list.

After visiting eight more towns Mlle. Lind returned to New York and gave fourteen concerts there, and her ninety-third, and last with Mr. Barnum, was at Philadelphia on May 9, 1851.

By this time both parties were tired out with the constant exertion and excitement, and were quite ready to end the contract, though to Mlle. Lind it meant the payment of a forfeit of 32,000 dollars. Thus the great venture ended with their friendship unimpaired, and Mlle. Lind admitted to Mr. Barnum later on that she had found it much more harassing to give the remaining concerts of her American trip on her own account.

The party that returned to New York was not the same that had started from there the previous autumn. Signor Salvi had succeeded Signor Belletti, and Mr.

AT THE REQUEST OF

THE MAYOR & CITIZENS OF TORONTO,

MD'LLE

JENNY LIND

WILL GIVE A

FAREWELL CONCERT

On Thursday Ev'ng, Oct. 23, 1851,

AT THE

ST. LAWRENCE HALL,

ASSISTED BY

SIGNOR SALVI,
MR. OTTO GOLDSCHMIDT,
SIGNOR E. BELLETTI,
AND
MR. JOSEPH BURKE.

PROGRAMME.

PART I.

FANTASIA—on Themes from La Sonnambula ....BELLETTI.
Clarionette—SIGNOR E. BELLETTI.

ROMANZA—"Una furtiva lagrima" ("l'Elisir d'Amore") DONIZETTI.
SIGNOR SALVI.

PRAYER—"Und ob die Wolke" (Der Freichutz). ....WEBER.
MD'LLE JENNY LIND.

FANTASIA—on Themes from Massaniello ....THALBERG.
MR. OTTO GOLDSCHMIDT

RECITATIVO—"Ah mie fedeli
ARIA—"Ma la sola" .... } (Beatrice di Tenda).....BELLINI.
MD'LLE JENNY LIND.

PART II.

FANTASIA—"Le Tremolo," Caprice on a Theme by Beethoven.............................DEBERIOT.
Violin—MR. JOSEPH BURKE.

CAVATINA—"Raimbaut" (Robert le Diable) ....MEYERBEER.
MD'LLE JENNY LIND.

REVERIE ....GOLDSCHMIDT.
Piano Forte—MR. OTTO GOLDSCHMIDT.

THE BIRD SONG.................................TAUBERT.
MD'LLE JENNY LIND.

CAVATINA—"In terra ci divisera" (Illustri Rivali)...MERCADANTE.
SIGNOR SALVI.

"JOHN ANDERSON MY JO'".....................Scotch Ballad.
MD'LLE JENNY LIND.

THE ECHO SONG ....Norwegian Melody.
MD'LLE JENNY LIND.

Doors open at 6½, Concert to commence at 8 o'clock.

☞ The price of Tickets has been fixed at $4 and $3. They will be for sale on Thursday Morning, Oct. 23rd, at 9 o'clock, at Messrs. A. & S. NORDHEIMER'S Music Establishment, King Street.

NOTICE.—This is the only Ticket Office, and Mr. BUSHNELL is the only authorized Agent for the sale of Tickets for Miss LIND'S Concert.

Henry Rowsell, Printer, King Street, Toronto.

Benedict had given place to Mr. Otto Goldschmidt, whom we already know as a friend of Mlle. Lind's. He was still young, but from the date of their meetings in Lübeck and Hamburg Mlle. Lind had appreciated his musical abilities and especially valued his powers as an accompanist. He had appeared also with her at the Brompton Hospital concert in 1848.

When the Barnum contract ended, Mlle. Lind continued her tour in a more leisurely fashion, and gave forty more concerts in seventeen towns, including Columbus (Ohio), Buffalo, and Toronto, and the last given in her maiden name was at Philadelphia on December 19, 1851.

On Mr. Barnum's ninety-five concerts with Mlle. Lind, the total receipts—of course exclusive of charity concerts—were 712,161 dollars, giving an average of 7,496, as only twenty-eight concerts fell short of 5500 dollars. The Wall Street prophets were therefore rather out in their reckonings! Mlle. Lind's share was 176,675 dollars, out of which she gave to New York charities the 10,000 dollars she received for the first two concerts. She gave twelve charity concerts on her tour. Under Barnum the price of tickets varied, to her great distress. The highest price paid at auction was 650 dollars at Providence, with Boston and Philadelphia running close at 625

JENNY LIND AT THE AGE OF 30.

From a Daguerrotype by Richards, Philadelphia.

dollars. The fixed price of from 3 to 7 dollars was never exceeded when Mlle. Lind gave her own concerts.

The programmes throughout consisted largely of famous Italian airs, such as from *Norma* and the *Sonnambula*; "Qui la voce" from *I Puritani*; airs by Mozart, Weber, and Meyerbeer; duets with Signor Belletti. The famous air with two flutes from Meyerbeer's *Das Feldlager in Schlesien* was in many a programme. In lighter vein she would sing Taubert's "Bird Song" in its terrible English translation, old English songs such as "Comin' through the Rye," "The Last Rose of Summer," and the Scottish songs "Auld Robin Gray" and "John Anderson, my Jo'," and few concerts were allowed to finish without some Swedish song, generally the "Echo Song." Mlle. Lind always accompanied herself in this song, but she never rose from her seat to invoke the echo; she merely turned towards the hall, and turned back to the piano as she played the last chord. Mlle. Lind never could have sung "Dixie" in America, as has been suggested, as the song was not written by Daniel Emmett till the time of the American Civil War, in 1859. Neither could she have worn a crinoline in 1851, as they were only introduced by the Empress Eugénie in 1857.

Towards the end of Mlle. Lind's tour in the autumn of 1851 her friendship with Otto Goldschmidt had become a vital one. Hers had been a lonely life, notwithstanding many friends and admirers, for she was, as we have seen, very reserved with strangers and desperately serious-minded, and the young Hamburger had many of the same characteristics. Small wonder that Mlle. Lind began to depend on her friend for sympathy and advice till a deep affection was mutually aroused and acknowledged.

Otto Goldschmidt came of a good Hamburg merchant family, and had early shown much musical talent, combined with considerable business astuteness. His mother was a Miss Schwabe, whose love of music encouraged her son to favour music rather than commerce, and in his fourteenth year we find him studying at the Leipzig Conservatoire under Hauptmann and Mendelssohn. Joachim and von Bülow were among his fellow-students, and the Hamburgers were very proud of their young musician when he appeared among them as a pianist at an early age. As an accompanist during the last months of the tour Mlle. Lind had found him so efficient that she had written to her guardian, Judge Munthe, that whether he accompanied her or she played for herself it was the same.

The marriage took place in the house of the banker, Mr. Sam Grey Ward in Boston on February 5, 1852, Bishop Wainwright officiating, and it caused great surprise and some resentment at the young man's good fortune, when the news leaked out, and the happy couple retired to Northampton for a brief honeymoon.

Mlle. Lind never contemplated losing control over the funds which she had worked so hard to earn, and before her marriage she drew up, in her own large, firm handwriting the draft of her marriage settlement. Under it she reserved to herself exclusive control over a portion of her fortune, the larger part constituting a common fund, over which her husband proved himself an able and faithful administrator. It need hardly be said that the private fund was used for charity, the only time Mme. Goldschmidt ever encroached upon it being for the purchase of her little Malvern house, years later.

On May 6, after their marriage, Mr. and Mme. Goldschmidt gave their first concert together at Northampton, where they had stayed since their marriage at Dr. Hall's hydro "Roundhill." This concert was for the benefit of the library for the Young Men's Institute, and Mr. Joseph Burke the violinist assisted. From there they went to New York, staying at Delmonico's, and they gave three farewell concerts in New York, on May 18 and 21 at the Metropolitan Hall, and on May 24 at Castle Garden. At these concerts Mr. Theodore Eisfeld conducted an orchestra of eighty performers, with Mr. Joseph Burke as leader.

The programme was the following, including a "Farewell to America," especially written for the occasion, as had been the "Welcome to America" which greeted Mlle. Lind's arrival twenty months before:

PROGRAMME OF LAST CONCERT IN AMERICA.

MONDAY EVENING, MAY 24, 1852.

PART I

OVERTURE, "Les deux journées" . . . *Cherubini*

CAVATINA, "Ah! per sempre" (*Puritani*) . . *Bellini*
SIGNOR C. BADIALI.

SCENA AND ARIA, "Casta Diva" (*Norma*) . *Bellini*
MME. JENNY GOLDSCHMIDT.

Last Movement of Concerto in G Minor . *Mendelssohn*
MR. OTTO GOLDSCHMIDT.

DUETTO, "Per piacere" (*Il Turco in Italia*) . *Rossini*
MME. JENNY GOLDSCHMIDT AND SIGNOR BADIALI.

PART II

OVERTURE, "Zampa" . . . . . . *Hérold*

TRIO for Soprano and two Flutes from *Camp of Silesia* . . . . . . *Meyerbeer*

MME. JENNY GOLDSCHMIDT.

Flutes: MESSRS. RIETZEL AND SEIDLER.

TARANTELLA . . . . *Thalberg*

Pianoforte: MR. OTTO GOLDSCHMIDT.

"Comin' through the Rye" . . . *Scotch Ballad*

"Echo Song" . . . . . . *Swedish Melody*

MME. JENNY GOLDSCHMIDT.

Largo al Factotum . . . . . . *Rossini*

SIGNOR C. BADIALI.

"Farewell to America," words by C. P. Cranch *Goldschmidt*

MME. JENNY GOLDSCHMIDT.

The Orchestra will be composed of 80 Performers.

Conductor: MR. THEO. EISFELD.

Leader: MR. JOSEPH BURKE.

CHAPTER XIV

1852–1856

On May 29, 1852, Mr. and Mme. Goldschmidt left New York in the same steamer, the *Atlantic*, with Captain West, that had brought Mme. Lind to the New World, and no doubt, with her hatred of turmoil, she was thankful that no Mr. Barnum was telling the world about her departure. The voyage was in every sense a calmer one, without winds and storms.

The Goldschmidts stayed at Fenton's Hotel in St. James's Street, and Mr. Goldschmidt was introduced to his wife's many friends, as well as meeting many of his own old friends, for he had been in London before and spoke English quite well, as so many Hamburgers do.

The rest of that summer was spent on pleasure trips in Switzerland and at Scheveningen, where Judge Munthe came to make the acquaintance of the man who had made his guardianship no longer necessary. Mr. Goldschmidt set himself to learn

Swedish, and subsequently made many journeys to Sweden to consult the old judge on business affairs.

In the autumn of this year the couple settled down at Dresden, where they remained domiciled for five years, during which time a son and a daughter were born to them. While in Dresden the Goldschmidts were meeting their many German friends, as well as keeping in touch with their now numerous English ones. These years showed no slackening in Mme. Goldschmidt's activities, and she continued her artistic career, singing in oratorio as well as in the music of Mendelssohn and Schumann. In the early half of 1854 she was on tour in Berlin, Leipzig, Vienna, and Pesth, but she was no longer harassed by the business side of her efforts, as her husband took all worries off her shoulders, and was her musical accompanist, as well as playing solo at many concerts, and conducting orchestras at others.

In the summer of 1854 we find the couple and their year-old son at Norderney, where the Hanoverian Royal family were also staying, and the Queen in her diary—which we are permitted to quote—noted many things, not only musical, which delighted her about Mme. Goldschmidt. She appears to have accompanied the King on riding expeditions, and to have greatly enjoyed them, and the Queen described the suppers, with music to follow, as well as the journey back together from Bremen by boat, when Mme. Goldschmidt burst into song over the beauties of the North Sea.

Nicholas Lind also came to Norderney to make the acquaintance of his daughter's husband and son. Mme. Lind had died soon after Mlle. Lind's arrival in America and therefore did not long enjoy the peace and comfort which had come to her with her daughters' help. Mr. Lind lived some years longer in Sweden with occasional visits to the Goldschmidt family in Germany.

In 1855, after giving concerts in Hamburg and Bremen, Mme. Goldschmidt made a brilliant tour from March to May in all the chief towns of Holland and Friesland, and in the May of that year she paid her first visit to the Rhenish Festivals at Düsseldorf.

These German tours were followed in the winter by a great tour of fifty-two concerts in England and Scotland, pleasantly inaugurated by a musical evening which Mr. and Mme. Goldschmidt were invited to give at Windsor Castle before the Queen and Court. Besides the orchestra there were no other performers, and Mme. Goldschmidt sang "On mighty pens," her husband's arrangement of Chopin's mazurkas for the voice, a song by Mendelssohn, and Taubert's "Cradle Song." This was rather a typical pro-

WINDSOR CASTLE,

FRIDAY, EVENING, DECEMBER 28TH, 1855.

OVERTURE—"Figaro," - - *Mozart*

ARIA—"On mighty pens" (*Creation*), - *Haydn*
Madame Goldschmidt.

CAPRICE—Piano Solo, - *Mendelssohn Bartholdy*
Mr. Goldschmidt.

RECUEIL de Mazourkas de F. Chopin, arranged
for Voice and Piano by - *Goldschmidt*
Madame Goldschmidt.

ETUDE } Piano Solo, - *Goldschmidt*
ALLEGRO } - - *J. S. Bach*
Mr. Goldschmidt.

LIEDER { "Die Sterne schau'n in Stiller Nacht," *Mendelssohn Bartholdy*
"Wiegenlied" (Cradle-song), *Taubert*
Madame Goldschmidt.

MARCH (Oberon), - - *C. M. von Weber*

gramme for Mme. Goldschmidt at that time, as it showed her in oratorio and lyrical music, with the vocalization of Chopin's difficult passages in between.

There was a further Royal Command concert at Buckingham Palace in the following May (1856).

The fifty-two concerts covered the ground between Cardiff and Exeter in the south, to Edinburgh and Glasgow in the north, with twenty-nine towns in between. The *Creation*, *Messiah*, and *Elijah* were the oratorios given, the remainder of the concerts were miscellaneous. They had their own orchestra, conducted by Mr. Benedict, and the rest of the party consisted of Messrs. Lablache, Weiss, Ernst, Sainton, Swift, and Piatti, with occasionally, for oratorio, Miss Dolby, who later married Mr. Sainton. John Mitchell of Bond Street was the agent for this tour and all other of Mme. Goldschmidt's engagements in England, and a testimony of their good relations is given in the fact that at his death he left mementos to both Madame and Mr. Goldschmidt.

It is very interesting to look through the old programmes and note the costs and arrangements of those days and the hire of halls no longer existing. The receipts, of course, depended on the size of the halls, the two smallest evidently being at Clifton and Winchester. The most interesting figures of the whole tour appear on April 30 when, at the Market Hall at Hanley, 2800 people must have been present, to judge by the tickets sold. Besides the dearer seats,

1483 were sold at 2s. 6d., the only occasion on which less than 5s. was ever charged; the usual prices being 1 guinea or 10s. 6d. At this concert Messrs. Weiss, Piatti, Ernst, and Ganz, as well as Mr. Goldschmidt, were in the programme, and Mme. Goldschmidt sang "On mighty pens," airs by Bellini, the Scotch song "John Anderson, my Jo," and the Swedish "Echo Song."

The tour had been interrupted in the month of March in order to give a concert in aid of the Nightingale Fund. Mr. Sidney Herbert, who was a friend of both Mme. Goldschmidt and Miss Florence Nightingale, had introduced the two ladies to each other, and had interested the former sufficiently in Miss Nightingale's great work in the cause of good nursing to induce her to give a concert in aid of funds. This concert took place in Exeter Hall on March 11, 1856, and resulted in a clear gain to the fund of £1872, Mr. and Madame Goldschmidt paying all expenses, and Messrs. Benedict and Lablache, as well as Mr. John Mitchell, waiving their fees. Reproductions of the cover and of the programme itself are shown on pages 182–3.

In recognition of their generosity, besides a special vote of thanks, the favourite sculptor of the day, Joseph Durham, A.R.A., was commissioned to make

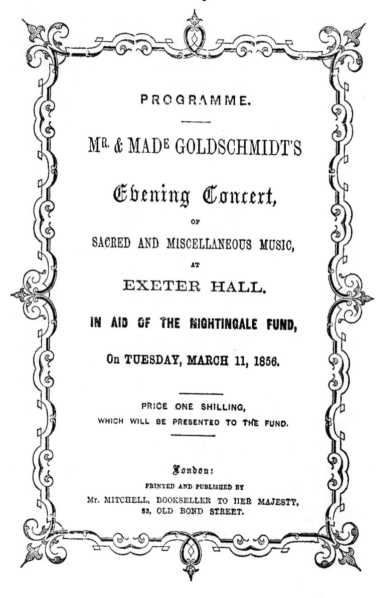

PROGRAMME.

MR. & MADE GOLDSCHMIDT'S

Evening Concert,

OF

SACRED AND MISCELLANEOUS MUSIC,

AT

EXETER HALL.

IN AID OF THE NIGHTINGALE FUND,

On TUESDAY, MARCH 11, 1856.

PRICE ONE SHILLING,
WHICH WILL BE PRESENTED TO THE FUND.

London:
PRINTED AND PUBLISHED BY
Mr. MITCHELL, BOOKSELLER TO HER MAJESTY,
33, OLD BOND STREET.

PROGRAMME.

Part I.

SYMPHONY (G Minor) . . . . *Mozart.*

HYMN for Soprano, Chorus & Organ, "*Hear my prayer, O God!*" *Mendelssohn Bartholdy.*
Madame JENNY GOLDSCHMIDT.

AIR, "*A te frà tanti affanni,*" Mr. SWIFT - (*Davidde Penitente*) *Mozart.*

CHORAL FANTASIA, Piano-forte, Orchestra and Chorus . . *Beethoven.*
Piano-forte, Mr. OTTO GOLDSCHMIDT.

The 130th PSALM, and other Passages of Scripture paraphrased, with the introduction of Martin Luther's Corale, "*Aus tiefer Noth,*" for Soprano Solo, Chorus and Orchestra . . . . . . *Otto Goldschmidt.*
INTRODUCTION.
AIR, "From the deep I cry," Madame JENNY GOLDSCHMIDT.
CHORUS, Martin Luther's Corale, "From depths of woe I cry to Thee."
INTERLUDE.
CHORUS, "See all the lilies."
DUETT, "From Thee are Grace and Mercy sought,"
Madame JENNY GOLDSCHMIDT and Mr. SWIFT.
CHORUS, "Then let thy soul await."
ARIOSO, "Though all the night," Madame JENNY GOLDSCHMIDT.
Clarionet Obligato, Mr. LAZARUS.
FINAL CHORUS, "Then in the Lord hope."
(First time of Performance.)

Part II.

OVERTURE to Shakespere's Play of "*The Tempest*" . . *Jules Benedict.*

ARIA with CHORUS, "*Squallida veste e bruna,*"
Madame JENNY GOLDSCHMIDT (*Il Turco in Italia*) *Rossini.*

CONCERTSTÜCK, for Piano-forte, with Orchestral Accompaniments *Weber.*
Piano-forte, Mr. OTTO GOLDSCHMIDT.

TRIO, for a Soprano Voice and Two Flutes, "*Hörst Du*"
Madame JENNY GOLDSCHMIDT:
Flutes, Messrs. R. S. PRATTEN & RÉMUSAT (*Camp of Silesia*) *Meyerbeer.*

PART SONG, "*When the West with Ev'ning glows*" . . . *Mendelssohn.*

SOLO, QUARTETT & CHORUS, "*Alziam gli evviva*" (*Euryanthe*) *Weber.*
Madame JENNY GOLDSCHMIDT,
Madame WEISS, Mr. SWIFT, and Signor F. LABLACHE.

MARCH & CHORUS from the "*Ruins of Athens*" . . . *Beethoven.*

a bust of Queen Victoria, which was presented to the Goldschmidts at a luncheon at the Mansion House two years later. A gift to Mme. Goldschmidt of a more intimate character was a little locket from Miss Nightingale, with her portrait inside and a grateful and affectionate inscription. We may perhaps be forgiven for anticipating events by relating how warmly Miss Nightingale wrote of this "early help to a fund which has grown into a large network of trained nurses for the sick" in a letter of condolence on Mme. Goldschmidt's death thirty years later.

Other interesting events of this year were a concert at Buckingham Palace, the programme of which is shown on p. 185, and a Command performance, the first in England, of Schumann's *Paradise and Peri.* It took place at the Philharmonic Society's rooms in Hanover Square on June 23, 1856, Sterndale Bennett conducting. Queen Victoria and Prince Albert were present, as was also King Oscar II of Sweden. Mme. Schumann was spending her first season in England and was also there. Mme. Goldschmidt, as we know, a great admirer of Schumann, frequently sang the airs from *Paradise and Peri*, but as a whole it had little vogue.

After these exhausting months it is no wonder that Mme. Goldschmidt was in need of a rest, which she

BUCKINGHAM PALACE.

FRIDAY, 30TH MAY, 1856.

Parte Prima.

SETTIMINO, " *Oh terror, oh smania,*"
Mesd[mes] Bosio, Novello, Viardot, e Didiée,
Sig. Gardoni, Mr. Weiss, e Hèrr Formes,
(Conte Ory) *Rossini.*

DUO, " *Amor possente nome,*"
Mad[e] Novello, e Mr. Sims Reeves, *(Armida)* *Rossini.*

AIR, " *Egli fù che a dir m' apprese,*"
Mad[e] Bosio, *(Arabi nelle Gallie)* *Pacini.*

RECUEIL de MAZOURKAS de F Chopin,
arranged for Voice and Piano, by . . *Otto Goldschmidt.*
Mr. and Mad[e] Goldschmidt

DUO, " *Qui dave mercè,*"
Mad[e] Bosio e Sig. Gardoni, *(Pastorale)* *Donizetti.*

AIR, " *Com' è bello,*"
Mad[e] Novello, *(Lucrezia Borgia)* *Donizetti.*

DUO, " *Allons, rentrez voici l'orage.*"
Mesd[mes] Goldschmidt e Viardot,
(La mère grand) *Meyerbeer.*

CORO, " *Signor del Ciel,*"
Mesd[mes] Novello, Bosio, Viardot, e Didiée,
Sig. Gardoni, Mr. Sims Reeves, Sig. Ronconi,
Mr Weiss, e Herr Formes, *(Eli)* *Costa.*

Parte Seconda.

OTTIMINO, " *All' idea,*"
Mesd[mes] Bosio, Novello, e Didiée,
Mr. Sims Reeves, Sig[ri] Gardoni e Ronconi,
Mr. Weiss, e Herr Formes, *(Mosè in Egitto)* *Rossini.*

NOCTURNE, ... *F. Chopin.*
and
LA TRUITE, by *Schubert*, for Piano, transcribed by *S. Heller.*
Herr Otto Goldschmidt

TRIO, " *Pensa e guarda,*"
Sig. Ronconi, Mr. Weiss, e Herr Formes,
(Margherita d'Anjou) *Meyerbeer.*

AIR, " *Squallida veste e bruna,*"
Mad[e] Goldschmidt, *(Turco in Italia)* *Rossini.*

DUO, " *Le ciel sourit au flot limpide,*"
Mesd[mes] Novello e Didiée, *(Le Zéphyr)* *Mendelssohn.*

VIEUX AIRS FRANÇAIS du 15 et 16 SIÈCLE.
Mad[e] Viardot.

CORO, " *Placido è il mar,*"
Tutti, *(Idomeneo)* *Mozart.*

At the Pianoforte, ... Mr. Costa.

took, together with a cure, at Kissingen. Sea-bathing at Norderney further rested her during the month of September, after which she returned via Hamburg and Berlin to Dresden for the winter.

In the following year the Goldschmidts received an offer from Mr. Barnum to revisit America, which offer they however declined. They remained, at the same, on terms of friendship with him for the rest of their lives, and he lived to take Mme. Goldschmidt's grandchildren to one of his Olympia exhibitions.

Some years later there was again an invitation to America from the Ladies' Committee of the United States Sanitary Commission, asking Mme. Goldschmidt to go and sing in a series of concerts in aid of a Voluntary Hospital Association affiliated to, but not of, a Government Department. There is rather a charming sentence in the letter of invitation from he President of the Committee, Mrs. Julia Fish. It runs:

The memories of your voice are still fresh in the hearts of Americans. Still more precious to them is the recollection that that voice was always exerted for benevolent and humane objects. The welcome that would await you is such as could only be given to Jenny Lind, whose harmonious notes have lingered in our ears, not only because they were delicious, but because they were the outpourings of a pure and gentle heart.

JENNY LIND.

From the bust by Christian Erickson in the Royal Opera House, Stockholm.

Ten years later, when her daughter grew up and was reputed to have a voice, Mme. Goldschmidt was once more invited to go to America, taking her daughter with her, but again this offer was not accepted.

In New York to-day there is a Jenny Lind Association which celebrated the centenary of her birth in 1920, and other towns in the United States did the same. It really would appear as if the above-quoted letter, though written in 1864, still represents a memory faithfully held in remembrance.

Sweden also does not forget her famous daughter, who remained a Swede at heart to the end, for her name is still constantly mentioned by word, and in print, in her own old country.

CHAPTER XIV

1858 TO THE END

AS so much of Mr. and Mme. Goldschmidt's life was now spent in England it seemed more practical, as well as being to their liking, to make their home in that country, where they now had a host of friends.

Mrs. Stanley, the wife of the Bishop of Norwich, had visited the Goldschmidts in Dresden when meeting her son on his return from Russia, and she was godmother to the little girl, the Goldschmidts' second child. On her return to England she was giving advice about an English nurse, and an English home, which was found first at Roehampton and then on Wimbledon Common among many new neighbours who soon became intimate friends. Mr. Goldschmidt took the earliest advantage of the new Naturalization Act and entered on many spheres of activity in London's musical world. His wife now called herself Mme. Lind-Goldschmidt and was desperately offended if addressed otherwise.

Her first big tour after the migration, took place in 1859 in the chief towns of Ireland, Joachim being with her party. She sang in the *Messiah* in Dublin, and Sir Charles Stanford has recorded the impression made on him as a boy of seven by her singing of the words " And they were sore afraid " in a whisper which went round the whole hall *pianissimo*.

In this little book we have purposely mentioned few of Mme. Goldschmidt's friends, as their name was legion, a fact of which we are constantly reminded nowadays, when few memoirs of Victorian days appear in which her name is not mentioned.

As a celebrity Mlle. Lind had met everyone worth knowing, and now in private life the Goldschmidts were warmly welcomed by their new neighbours, and their children grew up in a coterie of young friends.

This story opened with a reference to the nearness of age and attainment to power, of the two Queens, of England and of Song, and the parallel did not end there. For there was a certain similarity in the choice the two had made in their husbands. Both gentlemen were of German birth and both were endowed with German thoroughness; the one was a patron of the Arts which the other practised, and even in personal appearance they resembled each other in good looks.

These points of similarity could not escape their new Wimbledon neighbours, and they dubbed Mr. Goldschmidt "the Prince Consort of Song" until they found how much Mme. Goldschmidt resented that her husband should be put second, instead of first, in their home.

In 1859 Queen Victoria fired the opening shot which inaugurated the Volunteer Rifle Association's first meeting on Wimbledon Common near the old windmill, and during the weeks that it lasted, each year, there was much gaiety as well as business, and many pleasant evenings were spent in the camp by the residents as well as by visitors from London. There is a record of at least one evening, and there were probably more occasions when Mme. Goldschmidt, as the guest of Lord Elcho and the London Scottish, took part in a camp concert, singing in an open tent for all to hear; and we may be sure that she sang appropriately, the Scottish songs of which she was so fond.

When Mlle. Lind first came to London in 1847 she knew no English at all, and only very little when she toured in America. In the early copies of the oratorio airs which she used, we find her writing-in the phonetic spelling of words that troubled her. But she must have been taking lessons in English all the time; and in the first years of her marriage, when

meal	kilt	seed	beam
seal	spilt	deed	bean
deal	leave	steed	cheer
steel	leaf.	shield	beer
eel	leak	field	cheek
feel	sieve	neat	meek
kneel	lean	seat	weave
~~peal~~	~~loon~~	peer	weal
keen	leech	peeps	week.
reel	peach	keep	wean
key	peal	steeps	weep.
see	peace	speak	wheel
thee	peak	plea	whiff
me	free	three	which
he	freak	reach	whig
knee	seen	breach	whim
~~bean~~	bean	read	with
king	deem	ream	whisk
green	steem	reaps	will
thing	beam	reac	wing
ring	mint	wreath	fling
sing	milk	writhe	wind
spring	mist	yield	witch
sting	need	zeal	knit
		win	~~wink~~

she lived in Dresden, both she and her husband studied the language so thoroughly as to gain, eventually, complete mastery of it. We give a page of Mlle. Lind's writing, which shows how she studied the different ways of writing the same sounds.

After the birth of their third child, a boy, the Goldschmidts bought a piece of ground among the rhododendrons of Wimbledon Park, at the very spot to which Mlle. Lind had ridden with the Duke of Wellington during her London seasons, and Messrs. Cubitt built them a house with a great many tall Tudor chimneys. There was a splendid view across to the Crystal Palace, with a fine sight of the fireworks, long before the valley was built over as it is now. There was a good garden and paddock and a very old oak tree which no doubt sponsored the name "Oak-Lea," and this new home quickly became the centre of much hospitality. Arthur Sullivan had been welcomed in the family as the first Mendelssohn Scholar, long before he asserted his right to fame, and visitors from abroad, both in, and out of the musical world soon found their way to the house.

Mme. Albani must have come with one of her first introductions, on her arrival from Canada to gather her laurels, and she was sure of the sympathy of her elder sister in the realm of Song.

The hospitality savoured still of Swedish habits and cuisine, as Mme. Goldschmidt always had some Swedes in the household, who looked after the children when their parents were keeping their engagements, whether in England or abroad.

Up to the time of her marriage Mlle. Lind was always accompanied by a *dame de compagnie*, though there were only two of them during all that time. The first, as has been mentioned, was Mlle. Louis Johannsen, whose name appears on an early page as having been a boarder with Jenny's mother and her companion in flight when she left her mother's home. When she married she was succeeded by Mlle. Josefina Åhmansohnn, who remained with Mme. Goldschmidt after her marriage, and became housekeeper and "Auntie" to the children. Eventually she was one of Mme. Goldschmidt's pensioners and outlived her by some years.

In July, 1861, Mr. and Mme. Goldschmidt opened a busy period of concerts with one held, we are amusingly told, "by the obliging permission of the Earl of Dudley" at Dudley House in aid of the Society of Female Artists.

Then came a performance of the *Elijah* in Exeter Hall in aid of the church and school work at the Victoria Docks, and between that date and the end

PETERBORO' PROGRAMME—TUESDAY, APRIL 1

WENTWORTH ROOMS, PETERBORO'.

MR. & MADAME GOLDSCHMIDT'S

GRAND

Evening Concert,

Tuesday, April the 1st, 1862,

Commencing at EIGHT o'clock precisely.

VOCALISTS.

MADAME LIND-GOLDSCHMIDT,

MR. SIMS REEVES,

SIGNOR BELLETTI.

INSTRUMENTALISTS.

SOLO VIOLIN, MR. H. BLAGROVE. SOLO VIOLONCELLO, SIGNOR PIATTI.

PIANO FORTE AND CONDUCTOR, MR. OTTO GOLDSCHMIDT.

Reserved and Numbered Seats	One Guinea.
Family Tickets (admitting Four to ditto)	*Three Guineas.*
Reserved Seats (not Numbered)	Half-a-Guinea.

The Local Arrangements are under the superintendence of MR. CHADWELL, Peterboro', where Places may be secured, Tickets taken, and a Plan of the Rooms be seen.

PROGRAMME

FOR

TUESDAY EVENING, APRIL 1st, 1862,

Commencing at EIGHT o'clock precisely.

PART I.

FIRST MOVEMENT OF GRAND TRIO, B flat, for Piano, Violin and Violoncello . *Beethoven.*
Messrs. GOLDSCHMIDT, BLAGROVE and PIATTI.

SCENA ED ARIA, "*Care Compagne*" . . . . (*La Sonnambula*) *Bellini.*
Madame GOLDSCHMIDT.

DUETTO, "*O la bella,*" Mr. SIMS REEVES and Signor BELLETTI . . (*Betly*) *Donizetti.*

RONDO, for Voice and Violin Obbligato . . . . (*Il re Pastore*) *Mozart.*
Madame GOLDSCHMIDT.
Violin . . . . Mr. H. BLAGROVE.

FANTASIA on Themes from "*I Puritani*" . . . . *Piatti.*
Violoncello . Signor PIATTI.

ARIA, "*Il mio piano è preparato,*" Signor BELLETTI . . . (*La Gazza Ladra*) *Rossini.*

DUETTO, "*Rasserena o caro i rai*" . . . . (*Guglielmo Tell*) *Rossini.*
Madame GOLDSCHMIDT and Mr. SIMS REEVES.

PART II.

ADAGIO & RONDO, from Concerto in E . . . . *Mendelssohn.*
Violin . . Mr. H. BLAGROVE.

NEW SONG, "*Summer is sweet,*" Mr. SIMS REEVES . . . . *Lake.*

DUETTO, "*La dove prende amor ricetto*" . . . . (*Il Flauto Magico*) *Mozart.*
Madame GOLDSCHMIDT & Signor BELLETTI.

SCHERZO, "*Airs Baskyrs*" . . . . *Piatti.*
Violoncello . . . . Signor PIATTI.

BALLAD, "*My own, my guiding star*" . . . . (*Robin Hood*) *Macfarren.*
Mr. SIMS REEVES.

BARCAROLA, "*Sulla poppa,*" Signor BELLETTI . . . . *Ricci.*

{"JOHN ANDERSON MY JO"} Madame GOLDSCHMIDT . . . . {*Scotch Ballad.*
{ECHO SONG} {*Norwegian Melody.*

Conductor . . . . Mr. OTTO GOLDSCHMIDT.

ERARD'S PIANO-FORTE.

of the year the couple gave twenty-four concerts in the North of England and Scotland. The *Creation* was given in Edinburgh and the *Messiah* in Bradford, the other concerts consisting of miscellaneous items. In all these engagements Mme. Goldschmidt was singing while her husband conducted orchestras or accompanied his wife's singing, as well as playing pianoforte solos. The remainder of the party consisted of Messrs. Sims Reeves, Belletti, Blagrove, and Piatti.

We give a programme on pp. 194–5, indicative of the usual framing of these concerts and as showing the taste of the day and of the artists, but of course the actual items were constantly varied.

In January, 1862, the same party went on another tour, lasting till May. The opening concert at Derby on the 20th inst. is interesting by reason of the fact that it commenced with the National Anthem, sung by Mme. Goldschmidt in tribute to the Prince Consort, who had died a few weeks before. We give a reproduction of the black-edged programme which contains the additional stanza.

The tour embraced fifteen towns, and miscellaneous programmes were given on much the same lines as the previous year, but it ended with a performance of the *Creation* at Norwich and of the *Messiah* at Northampton.

DERBY.

January 20th, 1862.

The Concert

WILL BE COMMENCED WITH

THE NATIONAL ANTHEM,

SUNG BY

Madame GOLDSCHMIDT,

Mr. SIMS REEVES & Signor BELLETTI.

God save our gracious Queen,
Long live our noble Queen,
God save the Queen!
Send her victorious,
Happy and glorious,
Long to reign over us,
God save the Queen!

O Lord, our God, arise,
Scatter her enemies,
And make them fall!
Confound their politics,
Frustrate their knavish tricks,
On thee our hopes we fix,
O save us all!

Thy choicest gifts in store
On her be pleased to pour,
Long may she reign!
May she defend our laws,
And ever give us cause
To sing with heart and voice
God save the Queen!

ADDITIONAL STANZA.

Oh, Thou, whose chast'ning hand
Now lies on throne and land,
Oh, spare our Queen!
Thou, who has' sent the blow,
Wisdom and grace bestow,
Out of this cloud of woe!
God save the Queen!

Besides this tour Mr. and Mme. Goldschmidt gave three oratorios in London during the International Exhibition of 1862.

In March, 1863, England was deeply stirred and interested by the marriage of the Prince of Wales to the much-loved Danish Princess, and Mme. Goldschmidt was invited to sing a chorale of the Prince Albert's composing at the wedding in St. George's, Windsor, and take part in the festivities.

A great musical event of that year was Mr. Goldschmidt's revival of the *Allegro* and *Penseroso* of Handel to Milton's words, in which Mme. Goldschmidt took part, at St. James's Hall. The last time of its performance in its entirety had been under Sir George Smart at the Theatre Royal, Drury Lane, in 1813, and Mr. Goldschmidt took advantage of Sir George's offers of consultation as to his experience. The first of the two London performances was given in aid of the Royal Hospital for Incurables, and took place on May 1. Besides Mme. Goldschmidt, the singers included Mme. Lemmens Sherrington and Miss Lascelles, and Messrs. Montem Smith and Weiss, with a band and chorus of 250 performers, conducted by Mr. Goldschmidt. At the piano was Mr. Lindsay Sloper, and at the organ Mr. Hopkins, all well-known musicians of the day. The price of tickets was 1 guinea, 10s. 6d., and 7s. 6d. at the lowest.

In June of that year Mme. Goldschmidt was assisting at a *matinée* given by M. and Mme. Lablache in the Queen's Concert Rooms, Hanover Square. Others assisting were Mlle. Parepa, and Messrs. Thalberg and Piatti. Mme. Goldschmidt sang a Rossini duet with Signor Lablache, a Swedish melody, and Haydn's canzonetta, "My mother bids me bind my hair," which she had lately added to her repertoire. Thalberg played his own fantasy on *Mosé in Egitto.*

A month later Mme. Goldschmidt was again assisting at the same concert rooms for the benefit of Mlle. Louise Michal, with whom she sang duets. Other famous names on the programme are those of Mme. Trebelli and Signor Bettini (whom Mme. Trebelli afterwards married), Mr. Santley, and Mr. Charles Hallé. Mme. Goldschmidt sang an air from the "St. Cecilia's Ode" which also was revived that year, and she sang the air to Mr. Piatti's 'cello accompaniment.

Between these two *matinées* and the *Allegro* performance Mme. Goldschmidt had been across to Düsseldorf to sing in a miscellaneous concert, where two of her items had been the "*Re Pastore*" air, an air from the *Freischütz* and a part in the trio from *Fidelio*, an unusual item for her programmes.

So we get a good idea of the programmes to which, Mme. Goldschmidt was now devoting herself, and we see that her range of music was very wide.

In the Wimbledon days of the 'sixties and early 'seventies, music was the chief interest and recreation of the Goldschmidts' home. Mr. Goldschmidt was playing much Beethoven, Bach, and Chopin, and accompanying Mme. Goldschmidt in Schubert, Schumann, and Mendelssohn, of which she especially loved the latter's *Schilflied*, *Nachtlied*, and *Auf Flügeln des Gesanges*, and Schumann's *Dichter liebe* and *Stille Thränen*. The twilight hours were made lovely by the sound of the great artist singing, often to her own accompaniment, to her children and intimate friends. She would sing snatches of her old operatic airs, but chiefly songs by Lindblad, Kjerulf, and Taubert, invariably finishing with Schumann's *Wenn fromme Kindlein schlafen gehen*, a signal for closing the piano still kept up in the family. There was no lack of musical instruments in the house, as besides the precious little harmonium mentioned apropos of Christmas carols, there were three pianos and an organ!

Both Mr. and Mme. Goldschmidt made frequent visits to Sweden, taking their children with them on one occasion. They saw many old friends and were always kindly received by the Royal Family, and they still took counsel with the old judge on financial affairs. Besides this busy travelling life Mr. Goldschmidt had accepted the post of Vice-Principal of the Royal Academy of Music in Hanover Square under Sterndale Bennett as Principal, and these two gentlemen were also engaged together in the publication and translation (by Miss Catherine Winkworth) of German chorales, to collect which Mr. Goldschmidt made several journeys to his old Leipzig haunts and elsewhere. He had studied the organ in his student days under the famous Schneider, and now made use of his knowledge to undertake the post of Honorary Organist at the new church at West Hill, a mile or so from the Wimbledon Park home.

In the following years Mme. Goldschmidt would sing whenever a special occasion arose: for the Clergy Fund in London in 1865; at a Hamburg three-day festival in May, 1866. At this festival the *Messiah* was given in the great St. Michael's Church on the first day, the *St. Cecilia's Ode* on the second, and part of the *Paradise and Peri* and a mixed programme on the third day under Mr. Goldschmidt's conductorship. For the last time, in the month of June that year, Mme. Goldschmidt took part in a Düsseldorf Festival, and at its close we find her and her husband paying a visit to the King and Queen of Hanover, while the

Prussians were sitting at the gates demanding neutrality of the King during their war with Austria. Mme. Goldschmidt had a cold and could not sing, but other artists were performing, with the nervous consciousness of the situation which the King steadily ignored, and he was with difficulty persuaded to let the Goldschmidts catch the last train which left Hanover that night to rejoin their children at Düsseldorf.

Back in London, Mme. Goldschmidt took part in Arthur Sullivan's Grand Orchestral Concert in St. James's Hall on July 11, 1866, when she sang "Orpheus and his Lute" which he had dedicated to her, as well as "Sweet Day so Cool," still in MSS., and a Handel air.

The Hereford Festival Committee had commissioned Mr. Goldschmidt to write an oratorio for their 1867 festival, and he had chosen the story of Ruth for his subject. Mme. Goldschmidt took a deep interest in this work of her husband's and sang the soprano part on each of the five occasions on which it was given. The writing was of the Mendelssohn school, then being rather overshadowed by Brahms, Wagner, and the Moderns, and the critics did their best to kill it with faint praise.

We shall be anticipating somewhat if we say here

JENNY LIND.
From the bust by Joseph Durham, A.R.A.

that after the Kingston trial, with a verdict unpalatable to the Press, perhaps it was a bold move to give two performances of *Ruth* in the summer of 1871. But if the Press were silent of good words it made the independent judgment of the public and the rally of their fellow-artists of all the greater value to Mr. and Mme. Goldschmidt. There were two more performances of *Ruth* given in Düsseldorf and Hamburg, but a later invitation from Birmingham was not accepted.

Of the Goldschmidts' two sons, the elder had gone to Rugby in 1866, with Oxford and the Law to follow; the younger started with Mr. Waterfield's school at East Sheen, going eventually through Sandhurst to the Army, with the Staff College in between the South African and the Great Wars. The daughter was educated at home by an able Swiss governess who had previously taught the two sisters of John Addington Symonds.

While the elder boy was at Rugby his parents were often the guests of Dr. and Miss Temple at the School House. There is a story of rules being broken as the boys listened to the sound of Mme. Goldschmidt singing in the headmaster's drawing-room on one of these visits. But more than a story is the fact that on one wet Sunday afternoon Mme. Goldschmidt sang in the hall to the whole school, with the assistance of the first-rate amateur Mr. Arthur Duke Coleridge, whom she summoned from circuit for that purpose.

There were two songs composed by the Rugby music-master, Edwin Edwards, to Tennyson's words, "Late, late, so late," and "Sweet is true love," which Mme. Goldschmidt often sang in private. She, however, entirely failed to interest the poet himself when she sang them to him at Farringford, probably in 1875. Being as unmusical as Dean Stanley, he preferred his own rendering, with, as Mme. Goldschmidt used to describe, a drop in the voice at the end of each line!

In 1866 Mme. Goldschmidt began wintering in the South of France, at the Cannes which the venerable Lord Brougham had lately discovered. It was then a very different place from the now fashionable resort, and the inhabitants had not begun to shut their olive groves and wild tulips and anemones away from visitors.

The Goldschmidts had taken the Villa Alta, as its name denotes, high among the olive groves, and Mme. Goldschmidt used to delight in teaching the French to translate her name, so that when she sat among the olive-pickers singing to them, their "mais vous chantez tres-bien, Mme. Orfèvre" appealed strongly to her sense of humour. Both she and her young daughter sang in the choir of the first little English church, built in the corner of Mr. Woolfield's garden, and probably the other worshippers ceased their own singing to listen to that famous voice singing chants and hymns in the same way that they did twenty years later in the Little-Malvern church.

The only occasion on which Mme. Goldschmidt gave a concert in France was at Cannes in aid of the hospital, and the tickets could have been sold many times over. Apropos of this event, in his correspondence with Panizzi, Prosper Mérimée wrote from Cannes on March 16, 1866:

Parmi les agréments de Cannes j'aurai du, avant tout, vous parler de Jenny Lind, avec qui j'ai diné l'autre jour, et qui a chanté, sinon avec sa voix d'autrefois, du moins avec un filet délicieux. Elle est très-bonne femme, et n'a pas la vice que Horace reproche aux chanteurs : " Ut nunquam indicant animum cantare rogati." Elle va donner ici un grand concert pour les malades de l'hôpital. Le mal c'est qu'il n'y a pas de malades; dans ce pays tout le monde se porte bien.

Those happy Cannes winters, with the quiet intercourse of many interesting friends, were interrupted by the Franco-German War, and the winter of 1871–1872 was spent in Florence, where Mme. Goldschmidt at last fulfilled her desire to study the Italian painters in Italy, though of course during the years she had spent in Dresden she had learnt much in the galleries there.

But we must go back a few months to the March of 1871 when Mr. and Mme. Goldschmidt had decided at last to assert their good name in a court of law. At the time of the marriage in America we made use of the words "surprise and some resentment" at the good fortune of the man whom Mlle. Lind had chosen for her husband. During the ensuing years that this marriage had prospered, poisoned darts had been frequently aimed at Mr. Goldschmidt from the least reputable of the American journals and had been steadily ignored. When, however, in 1871 English newspapers copied these libellous paragraphs it was time to take notice, and the printers were sternly brought to account at Kingston Assizes before Lord Chief Justice Cockburn and a special jury. Sir John Duke Coleridge, afterwards Lord Chief Justice, Mr. Charles Pollock, and the Hon. Alfred Thesiger, all eminent lawyers, appeared for the plaintiffs, and in the witness-box Mme. Goldschmidt asserted that not only had her husband not squandered her fortune, as the libels declared, but under his careful management her financial position was materially improved. Among other witnesses the aged 9th Earl of Leven and Melville testified to his knowledge of the couple's happiness and concord, during the twelve years that they had been his neighbours.

After the excitement and worry of the trial had died away Mr. and Mme. Goldschmidt and their children spent some weeks in Bavaria, where the Ammergau Passion Play was being given. Owing to the Franco-Prussian War there had been a postponement from the previous year, and Josef Meyer, who impersonated the Christ, had been specially permitted to keep his hair long when soldiering. Mme. Goldschmidt thoroughly enjoyed the simple life which the accommodation of the village made necessary, and the play itself impressed such a nature as hers greatly. Insomuch, that after settling her family in the village of Partenkirchen, she returned by herself to witness a second performance. In considerable contrast must have been her feelings some weeks later on hearing Wagner's *Lohengrin* for the first time in Munich, with Vogl as the Knight of the Grail.

Mr. and Mme. Goldschmidt and their three children were leading a full social life, with frequent visits to Scotland and the Lake country as well as abroad, and Mme. Goldschmidt often went to Sweden to see her old friends. She also took the waters at Wiesbaden as a relief from the rheumatism which now troubled her, and in the intervals of her cure she took great pleasure in initiating her daughter in the operas performed at the first-rate Opera House, where performances were both cheap and early, as they began at 6 o'clock and cost about 4s. a seat. As the result of rheumatism Mme. Goldschmidt felt the cold in England very much, and the Indian shawls in which she now wrapped herself became familiar articles of her dress. Queen Victoria had given her two splendid specimens, which she wore on special occasions, but she had several others, the oldest and most cherished of which was by her direction laid in her coffin. She was never a good dresser, and selected materials more for their quality than for their beauty.

It had now become evident that with their children growing up and their own ever-increasing interest in musical and social life in London, it would be more convenient to leave their happy Wimbledon home and live in London itself, and in 1875 Mr. and Mme. Goldschmidt rented a furnished house before settling on the purchase of a house of their own in South Kensington.

Sir William Sterndale Bennett, the Principal of the Royal Academy of Music, which was then in Tenderden Street, Hanover Square, died after a very short illness on February 1, 1875, and Mr. and Mme. Goldschmidt attended his funeral in Westminster Abbey. He had been a great friend and ally of Mr. Goldschmidt's, and with his death the latter retired from active service at the Royal Academy, though remaining on the governing body, and he did a good deal of examining work for various musical institutions.

He belonged to the Royal College of Organists and to the Royal College of Music on its foundation, and he was a Member of the Swedish Royal Academy of Music and the London Company of Musicians. He was, moreover, a keen member of the Madrigal Society, and delighted in its meetings, long before the inception of the last big musical interest of his life, the Bach Choir. This really grew out of a little private choir of twenty-two voices formed from the best amateurs of the day who met once a week at Mr. Goldschmidt's house under his bâton to sing little-known *a capella* works by Palestrina, Orlando Lasso, Pearsall, Weekes, etc., as well as Bach motetts.

Mr. Arthur Coleridge, the tenor, a man of many friends, was at that time greatly interested in Bach's B Minor Mass, of which he had heard portions, and, fired by his enthusiasm, the little choir started the project of increasing their numbers in order to study and give the first performance in England of this supreme work, under the training and conductorship of Mr. Goldschmidt. With rapidly increased numbers the choir soon outgrew the Goldschmidts' house, and the use of Mr. and Mrs. Freake's fine music-room at Cromwell House was gratefully accepted, before the final migration to the South Kensington Museum's lecture hall. Mr. Goldschmidt travelled to Germany to consult authorities on the Mass, and wrote out from them some extra band parts which he used at all his performances, and on November 19, 1875, sixty-five amateurs attended the first practice at Mrs. Freake's house. Mme. Goldschmidt herself led the soprani, and coached the ladies in the difficult music at her own house as well, surely a unique instance of a great singer's enthusiasm for a great master.

The whole winter was devoted to the study of the Mass in preparation for its first performance in its entirety, in England, at St. James's Hall on April 26, 1876, when the Bach Choir took its place in the musical history of London.

On March 21, 1885, the Choir celebrated the bicentenary of Bach's birth in a festival performance of the B Minor Mass with greatly augmented numbers at the Albert Hall. The chorus and orchestra numbered over 600, and the soloists were Miss Anna

Williams, Madame Patey, Mr. Edward Lloyd, and Signor Foli, with Mr. Goldschmidt conducting.

After ten years' work, both conducting and editing the works performed, Mr. Goldschmidt resigned the conductorship and Sir Charles Stanford was appointed to succeed him.

We think that interested readers will not have failed to appreciate, since the entry of Mr. Goldschmidt into this story, the important part he plays in it. In her early letters Mlle. Lind constantly wrote of her loneliness and dislike of having to battle with the business of life. From the moment of her marriage, which was one of genuine affection and sympathy

ST. JAMES'S HALL.

WEDNESDAY EVENING, APRIL 26th, 1876,
AND
MONDAY EVENING, MAY 8th, 1876.

J. SEBASTIAN BACH'S

MASS IN B MINOR

(First Time of Performance).

The following Noblemen and Gentlemen have formed themselves into a Committee to ensure an efficient Performance of Sebastian Bach's Great *Mass in B Minor*.

THE RIGHT HON. LORD COLERIDGE.
(Lord Chief Justice of the Court of Common Pleas.)
THE RIGHT HON. LORD MONTEAGLE.

W. H. GLADSTONE, Esq., M.P.
C. J. FREAKE, Esq.
GEORGE GROVE, Esq.
OTTO GOLDSCHMIDT, Esq.
W. H. EVANS, Esq.
LIONEL BENSON, Esq.
DR. MONK.
G. E. MAUDE, Esq.
KELLOW J. PYE, Esq.
DR. STAINER.
J. EDW. STREET, Esq.
E. P. WOLFERSTAN, Esq.
E. WINGFIELD, Esq., *Hon. Treas.*
A. D. COLERIDGE, Esq., *Hon. Sec.*

THE CHORUS

consisting of distinguished Amateurs, Ladies and Gentlemen, will be assisted by members of the Choirs of St. Paul's Cathedral, St. George's Chapel, Windsor, etc.

THE ORCHESTRA

Will be complete, comprising many eminent professors.

The Soli parts will be rendered by the following Artistes:

Madame LEMMENS-SHERRINGTON,
Madame PATEY,
Mr. W. H. CUMMINGS,
Signor FEDERICI.

Leader, - Herr STRAUSS.

Organist, Mr. THOMAS PETTIT.
Conductor, - Mr. OTTO GOLDSCHMIDT.

Sofa Stalls and First Row in Balcony, - 10s. 6d.
Area and Balcony, Reserved, 7s., *Unreserved*, 5s.
Admission, - 3s.

Tickets may be obtained at
Mr. Mitchell's Royal Library, 33, Old Bond Street;
Messrs. Stanley Lucas Weber & Co., 84, New Bond Street;
Messrs. Chappell, 50, New Bond Street; Messrs. Keith, Prowse, & Co., Cheapside; Mr. A. Hays, Royal Exchange Buildings; and at Mr. Austin's Ticket Office, St. James's Hall.

Seats can be secured for both Performances, and any balance that may remain over the expenses will be devoted by the Committee to Public Purposes.

*** *Doors open at Seven o'clock; to commence at Eight o'clock precisely.*

on both sides, her husband had shielded her from worry and annoyance, even to the diplomatic handling of unwanted visitors, and he spared her from all possible fatigue on the great tours which Mr. and Mme. Goldschmidt took together for over fifteen years of their married life. Mr. Goldschmidt's own musical achievements were not small, and his personal influence among friends and colleagues was almost as great, for he was looked up to with real respect for his knowledge in music and his tact in life. He was devoted to England and the English, loving its institutions and having a keen insight into its politics.

From Sweden he had received the orders of the Vasa, and the gold medal of the Polish Star, conferred by the King, but the distinction which gave him most pleasure was his election in 1876 to the Athenæum Club under Rule II.

Mr. Goldschmidt had always interested himself in musical education in England, and his sound knowledge as well as his independent position made him a valuable authority, freely consulted by fellow-musicians for the twenty years that he survived Mme. Goldschmidt. He took a deep interest in his daughter's musical children, especially the younger boy, to whom he gave piano lessons, and his grandson has vivid recollections of his teaching of Bach,

Photo: Downey.

Jenny Lind-Goldschmidt.
Sept. 3d 1880.

Beethoven, Schumann, and Chopin, and the lucidity of his readings when consulted by prominent musicians, at whose visits he was privileged to be present.

We have rather digressed in our chronicle and need to return to the life which Mme. Goldschmidt was leading in the midst of her family and a host of friends who came to the house at 1 Moreton Gardens. She had very good ground-floor rooms adapted to parties and the little dances that she gave now that her children were grown up. At these dances many a young man would seek a few turns with Mme. Goldschmidt, who had always loved dancing but had denied herself the pleasure for the sake of her voice, and the attendance at these dances was a generous medley from the Crown Prince of Sweden downwards. For the Swedish Royalties never failed to visit Mme. Goldschmidt when they came to London, and our own Royalties had always distinguished the Goldschmidts with their friendship.

The last few times that Mme. Goldschmidt sang for charity were hardly of a public nature, being, with the exception of the very last, all in private houses at guinea tickets.

In 1871, as noted earlier in our pages, together with Signor Piatti, she assisted at a *matinée* which

Mme. Schumann gave on April 20 in a private house, 14 Hyde Park Gate, and it is nice to find the two old friends making music together once more. Mme. Schumann played a Beethoven Sonata, two Chopin pieces, and some of her husband's music. The latter also was the composer of Piatti's solo. Mme. Goldschmidt sang two songs of her husband's and the "Cavatina" from the *Freischütz.*

In 1873 Mme. Goldschmidt sang at Northumberland House, Trafalgar Square, before the building was swept away to make room for the avenue of its name and the lion with outstretched tail was banished to Sion House, Twickenham; in 1877 she sang in aid of Lady Layard's Turkish Refugee Fund; in 1878 she helped her turbulent devotee, Mlle. Janotha, by singing one number to Mr. Guerini's violin obbligato at a private concert; and yet again she sang, by Princess Christian's request, on behalf of the Albert Institute at Windsor in May, 1880. She maintained the quality and timbre of her voice to the very end of her life, though long having ceased to live the life of a singer. The very last time that Mme. Goldschmidt ever sang in public was in 1883 under amusing circumstances. She had lately bought a little house in a delicious spot right on the Malvern Hills, and when arriving by train for her summer holiday

Photo: Tilley, Ledbury.

WYND'S POINT.

Mme. Goldschmidt's Malvern home.

the porter who handled her luggage calmly asked her if she would sing at the annual Railwaymen's Benefit Concert. Mme. Goldschmidt was so much amused at the manner of the request that she accepted and actually did sing to an overflowing audience.

Of the three London concert halls in which Mme. Goldschmidt is mentioned as having sung, none remains.

The Strand Palace Hotel now occupies the site of Exeter Hall, which was a gloomy building, used for May Meetings of Churchmen before the erection of the Church House in Westminster, as well as for concerts.

In Hanover Square, shops at the corner of Hanover Street, replace the old concert hall where we have described the first performance in England of Schumann's *Paradise and Peri.*

And, lastly, the St. James's Hall, of excellent acoustics, and memories of the famous Victorian Saturday Popular Concerts; where the muffin-bell chimed in with Paderewski, and an occasional strain from the Christy Minstrels on the ground-floor encroached on the classics of the upper hall, has given place to the Piccadilly Hotel.

The St. James's Hall was built in 1857, and Mr. Goldschmidt would appear to have been interested in it from start to finish, for he bought a £100 Founders' share when it was being built, and he played the accompaniments for his granddaughter, when she sang there at a concert given by the Magpie Madrigal Society, under Mr. Lionel Benson, in 1903.

After the marriage of her daughter Mme. Goldschmidt felt the need of more occupation, and at the request of King Edward, then still Prince of Wales, she accepted the post of first Professor of Singing in the Royal College of Music then being inaugurated in South Kensington, with Sir George Grove as its Principal. This was in 1883, before the new college was built, and what is now the College of Organists was far too small a home. So the fortunate pupils whom Mme. Goldschmidt had taken, attended classes in her own large drawing-room in Moreton Gardens. Sir Charles Stanford has described Mme. Goldschmidt's attendance at the examination for candidates before the Board of Professors. There being no piano in the room, Mme. Goldschmidt would reel off terrifying passages to the amazement of the examiners and no doubt the anguish of the girls, who were expected to imitate them.

Mme. Goldschmidt also compiled a memorandum of her ideas for the proper training of a singer, no doubt with the memory of her own young days, plus her own great experience. But the time was not then ripe for so all-embracing a curriculum, though the ensuing years may have added to the original plans.

But the fatigue of teaching was too great for Mme. Goldschmidt's already enfeebled health, and she did not continue the undertaking for more than three years. Her summers were spent in her Malvern home, and her last winter found her once more at Cannes, where she had the unpleasant experience of the Ash-Wednesday earthquake in 1887. She was able to return to England and spend her last summer on earth with her family round her at Malvern, and she passed away on All Souls' Day at the comparatively early age of sixty-seven. She greeted the sunshine which came into her room on the last morning of her life with some bars of Schumann's *Sonnenschein*.

On the news of Mme. Goldschmidt's death there was an extraordinary outburst of regret and sympathy from all over England and other countries, and the newspapers devoted much space to her life and successes. We might almost feel that so much praise as Jenny Lind received all her life becomes monotonous did we not remember that her great achievements were won by hard work and unremitting effort, as well as by force of character.

Her funeral at Great Malvern was attended by

representatives of Royalties as well as of the Arts, and by many friends, and a last tribute was paid to her memory when the Dean of Westminster acceded to a widely signed petition for a memorial in the Abbey. This was placed in Poets' Corner beneath that of Handel, of whose music she was so great an interpreter.

Truly it may be said: Jenny Lind began as a fashion and remains as a tradition.

THE WESTMINSTER ABBEY MEMORIAL.

INDEX

Printed in Great Britain at
The Mayflower Press, Plymouth. William Brendon & Son, Ltd.

F 25.826

Opera Biographies

An Arno Press Collection

Albani, Emma. **Forty Years of Song.** With a Discography by W. R. Moran. [1911]

Biancolli, Louis. **The Flagstad Manuscript.** 1952

Bispham, David. **A Quaker Singer's Recollections.** 1921

Callas, Evangelia and Lawrence Blochman. **My Daughter Maria Callas.** 1960

Calvé, Emma. **My Life.** With a Discography by W. R. Moran. 1922

Corsi, Mario. **Tamagno, Il Più Grande Fenomeno Canoro Dell'Ottocento.** With a Discography by W. R. Moran. 1937

Cushing, Mary Watkins. **The Rainbow Bridge.** With a Discography by W. R. Moran. 1954

Eames, Emma. **Some Memories and Reflections.** With a Discography by W. R. Moran. 1927

Gaisberg, F[rederick] W[illiam]. **The Music Goes Round.** 1942

Gigli, Beniamino. **The Memoirs of Beniamino Gigli.** 1957

Hauk, Minnie. **Memories of a Singer.** 1925

Henschel, Horst and Ehrhard Friedrich. **Elisabeth Rethberg:** Ihr Leben und Künstlertum. 1928

Hernandez Girbal, F. **Julian Gayarre:** El Tenor de la Voz de Angel. 1955

Heylbut, Rose and Aimé Gerber. **Backstage at the Metropolitan Opera** (Originally published as **Backstage at the Opera**). 1937

Jeritza, Maria. **Sunlight and Song:** A Singer's Life. 1929

Klein, Herman. **The Reign of Patti.** With a Discography by W. R. Moran. 1920

Lawton, Mary. **Schumann-Heink:** The Last of the Titans. With a Discography by W. R. Moran. 1928

Lehmann, Lilli. **My Path Through Life.** 1914

Litvinne, Félia. **Ma Vie et Mon Art:** Souvenirs. 1933

Marchesi, Blanche. **Singer's Pilgrimage.** With a Discography by W. R. Moran. 1923

Martens, Frederick H. **The Art of the Prima Donna and Concert Singer.** 1923

Maude, [Jenny Maria Catherine Goldschmidt]. **The Life of Jenny Lind.** 1926

Maurel, Victor. **Dix Ans de Carrière, 1887-1897.** 1897

Mingotti, Antonio. **Maria Cebotari,** Das Leben Einer Sangerin. [1950]

Moore, Edward C. **Forty Years of Opera in Chicago.** 1930

Moore, Grace. **You're Only Human Once.** 1944

Moses, Montrose J. **The Life of Heinrich Conried.** 1916

Palmegiani, Francesco. **Mattia Battistini:** Il Re Dei Baritoni. With a Discography by W. R. Moran. [1949]

Pearse, [Cecilia Maria de Candia] and Frank Hird. **The Romance of a Great Singer.** A Memoir of Mario. 1910

Pinza, Ezio and Robert Magidoff. **Ezio Pinza:** An Autobiography. 1946

Rogers, Francis. **Some Famous Singers of the 19th Century.** 1914

Rosenthal, Harold [D.] **Great Singers of Today.** 1966

Ruffo, Titta. **La Mia Parabola:** Memorie. With a Discography by W. R. Moran. 1937

Santley, Charles. **Reminiscences of My Life.** With a Discography by W. R. Moran. 1909

Slezak, Leo. **Song of Motley:** Being the Reminiscences of a Hungry Tenor. 1938

Stagno Bellincioni, Bianca. **Roberto Stagno e Gemma Bellincioni Intimi** *and* Bellincioni, Gemma, **Io e il Palcoscenico:** Trenta e un anno di vita artistica. With a Discography by W. R. Moran. 1943/1920. Two vols. in one.

Tetrazzini, [Luisa]. **My Life of Song.** 1921

Teyte, Maggie. **Star on the Door.** 1958

Tibbett, Lawrence. **The Glory Road.** With a Discography by W. R. Moran. 1933

Traubel, Helen and Richard G. Hubler. **St. Louis Woman.** 1959

Van Vechten, Carl. **Interpreters.** 1920

Wagner, Charles L. **Seeing Stars.** 1940